infinite
INSPIRATIONS

Creative & daring responses to life's challenges

D Coleman

The Daring Doctor!

David Coleman & Lenny Dave

Edited by
Diane Tenaglia
dianetenaglia@gmail.com

Layout by
Dani Hiar, Ed.D.
dani.hiar@gmail.com

ISBN: 198125871X
ISBN-13: 978-1981258710

The MasterMind Speaking/Coaching Weekend™
(hosted by David Coleman & Lenny Dave)

Discover Your Purpose… Define Your Passion…
and Develop the Methods to Deliver Your Message.

This book is the direct result of a collaborative effort by participants in the inaugural MasterMind Speaking/Coaching Weekend (2017).

This workshop/seminar/training is dedicated to helping speakers and authors master their message, hone their public speaking skills and learn from other speakers and authors who have gathered to
do the same. What message do you want to share with the world? Here is your opportunity to pursue it.

Reach out – Communicate – Share – Listen – Learn – Improve – Grow… and savor the meaningful, new friendships you make along the way.

Interested in attending the next MasterMind Speaking/Coaching Weekend? Interested in hosting such an experience in your community or your region of the country?
Please contact: David@DavidColemanSpeaks.com.

As this book is a compilation, each contributing author is solely responsible for the content of their chapter. Each author has provided their own personal contact information.

CONTENTS

ABOUT THE COVER

Balloons? Why do we hold onto some of them so tightly while releasing others willingly to fly away? Do our balloons necessarily convey a sense of happiness, or might they mean something entirely different to you; something not quite so pleasant or joyous?

In one sense, we all are holding onto balloons. For the purpose of this book, they represent moments in our life, past and present. They are both good and bad, positive and negative, happy and sad, hurtful and helpful. Perhaps these balloons are warm and loving thoughts of people and places in our past. If so, we cling to them with a firm and steady grip, never letting go. They are our guideposts, our rock, our foundation. With emotional reverence, we look to them from time to time, whether they are present or now only a cherished memory. They help to center and uplift us when we weaken. They set us on the right path when we begin to stray.

Then again, these balloons may also represent our challenges, our problems, our dark places, our issues, our so-called "baggage." Perhaps these balloons are toxic moments or poisonous people who have weighed us down, slowed our progress and prevented us from enjoying and appreciating the sweetness that life has to offer. These balloons keep us looking backward instead of forward. Seeing even the possibility of a brighter tomorrow is eclipsed by their lurking, daunting shadow.

In creatively and boldly responding to life's challenges, how long we choose to hold onto our balloons, figuratively speaking, is often up to us. The colorful, abstract winds of fate represent something much bigger than us. They might take some of those balloons up, up and away… if we would just choose to let go of them. And, if we did let go, destiny's brisk breeze could perhaps take some of them on a skyward journey elsewhere, somewhere far beyond the horizon, beyond our control and beyond our imagination. Best of all, in "letting go," they are no longer ours to possess; they no longer impede or influence us. Once, they did touch our life, but now we are free of them.

And what of those balloons that do not blow away as soon as we choose to release them? They are all dealt with in time. Ask any parent cleaning up their young child's room. Many balloons inevitably end up as a deflated piece of rubber on the floor, in the corner or under the bed. How much better, then, might it have been to let them float away to know the simple joy of being a balloon!

1 Lost and Found
Lenny Dave

At times, it can be as unmistakably obvious as the incessant pounding of a jackhammer. Other times, it can be as elusive and subtle as the gentle breeze on a warm summer evening. The word "unpredictable" describes it well. Perhaps you've noticed this, too. I have—and more than once; especially over these past several years.

The "it" to which I am referring is Life and the uncanny way it has of teaching us lessons that no conventional classroom could ever convey, not even in the most comprehensive curriculum. No gray-haired professor, no fresh-faced graduate student could ever explain it more clearly and powerfully than the way our own collection of day-to-day experiences does. Our secret stash of life's meaningful moments etches the message into our consciousness. And sometimes, it implants itself on a much deeper level.

Recognizing, accepting and truly learning from these life lessons only happens when we, ever the student, are ready and receptive. I am reminded of the popular proverb, "When the student is ready, the teacher will appear." Often, though, the student is not ready and the decisive moment of learning or enlightenment is lost.

By being ready and receptive, I mean the following: when we begin to see and not just look, when we begin to listen and not just hear, when we begin to talk less and observe more, when we are not just there, but we are also present. It would stand to reason, then, that the more years we have under our belt, the more opportunity we have to learn these life lessons.

Let me ask you—or perhaps you should ask yourself—Do you pay attention? Do you observe? Are you aware? Are you present? Do you see? Do you listen? Are your antennae sensitized? Are you introspective? Are you appreciative? Are you grateful?

To better understand my perspective on this, here, in one phrase, is my professional identity; I am a writer who speaks and a speaker who writes. That's it. I've been doing both for over four decades. In communicating thoughts and ideas through the written and spoken word, I am continually challenged to touch my audience and connect with my readers. In person, my goal is to create a shared experience—a moment. Often, I can add the warmth of a handshake or holding someone's hand, enhancing the moment with a sincere smile and perhaps brief but genuine conversation. On the printed page, my goal is to plant a seed, to awaken, to stimulate, to engage, to inspire, to tell a story.

Even though I am not a doctor, my intention is to perform successful surgery on the human spirit. For whatever gifts I have been given by the Divine, and for whenever and however I attempt to share them, I am most grateful and appreciative for the talent I have acted upon and cultivated over these many years. My career has evolved, twisted and turned. It has been anything but a straight line from where I started to where I am now. And, it has been anything but easy. But, it has been my career… my life… and I accept ownership of it.

One of my favorite audiences these days consists of active senior adults, the "Over 55" crowd. However, that generic, demographic label is simply too broad. Some seniors are very much on-the-go; some are, quite frankly, nearly gone.

Some recent retirees and their significant other still play tennis or golf, go to the theater and the symphony, dine in fine restaurants, delight in creating in the kitchen, work in the garden, play bridge, play mahjong, and still drive their car from here to there without a care. These seniors have found that life, even with all of its medicated aches and pains, isn't so bad. And, it sure beats the alternative.

By contrast, other seniors are alone, literally and/or figuratively. Perhaps they have lost their beloved. Perhaps they are losing them now, watching them slip away, day-by-day. Some seniors are aided by canes and walkers (yes, the ones with the brightly colored tennis balls covering the base of the metal feet). Some seniors drive scooters like Mario Andretti and are hell-bent on getting to wherever they are going, "Beep-Beep!" And, some seniors are now dependent on wheelchairs and an ever-present aide who sits with them, takes them from room-to-room, to the daily activity, to the dining room…or to the doctor. Their days of living independently have long since passed. And, they realize that waking up tomorrow is no guarantee.

I interact with my senior audiences at various stages along their geriatric journey. For some in my audience, their measurable eyesight may have been diminished, but their broader vision has been sharpened by their collective years of experience; wisdom that comes with age. What really matters to them is now clearly in focus.

Above all, what I have learned from interacting with my senior audiences is an expansive sense of empathy and compassion. In sharing countless, nostalgic memories of the great comedians who made them laugh for decades, I create a positive emotional experience for them. Seeing and hearing about Charlie Chaplin, Laurel & Hardy, Jack Benny, Bob Hope, George Burns & Gracie Allen, Milton Berle, Lucy, Sid Caesar, Red Skelton, Jackie Gleason and so many more, never gets old for them, or for me. It always brings a smile to their face, laughter to their lungs, and happiness to their hearts. I take them back in time so they can relive the past while appreciating it, perhaps even more so, in the present.

This positive, emotional connection the audience experiences is priceles. Sure, medications may relieve or lessen their pain, but humor and laughter provide a healthy dose of joy—a booster shot of happiness. Norman Cousins, author of Anatomy of an Illness as Perceived by the Patient said it best, "The more laughter there is, the higher the quality of life. And, the higher the quality of life, the greater the will to live."

Toward the end of my program, I usually share the following thought, hopefully encompassing everyone in the room. I get it—to the best of my ability, I understand—I know you. I know that you have raised families and run households. You endured and survived The Great Depression. You have sweated and sacrificed. You fought in wars a world away (and many of you still bear the visible or hidden scars to prove it). You worked in the factories and on the farms. You lived in the cities and the suburbs. Many of you started and have grown your own business, developed corporate empires and ruled over an industry. And, many of you have traveled far and wide, whether for business or pleasure, witnessing wonders (and collecting souvenir postcards to prove it). In short, each one of you has a fascinating life story to tell, though you may not have chosen yet to share it. You (and only you) are the sole storyteller of your life's tale and trail. For your children, grandchildren and for all of the generations to follow—document your life story. Let them know who you were, where you came from, what you did, what you experienced and what you learned along the way.

One particular night, one of those powerfully memorable moments presented itself to me. And, because my antennae are always super-sensitized before a show, I paid special attention to this moment as it unfolded over the course of the evening.

About 15 minutes before show time, an aide wheeled an older woman into the theater, carefully positioning her wheelchair in the front row so she could see and hear me better. With the emotionless task completed, the aide quickly disappeared. The woman in the wheelchair wore a yellow sweater, and a heavy one at that. A scotch plaid blanket covered her legs and torso. But, what struck me as odd was that she had on a pair of dark, wrap-around sunglasses. Yet, we were indoors and it was night; the sun had long since set.

Always interested in making the human connection with as many people in my audience as possible before a show, I slowly but confidently walked towards the woman, certain of at least extending a pleasant, "Hello!" And then, I noticed it. From whatever medical situation had befallen her (a stroke perhaps, or maybe the latter stages of Parkinson's), she sat there, quiet, motionless and seemingly non-responsive. She could not move her head; it was tilted slightly back and leaning a bit to the left. She could not move her arms; her left limb lay limp across her lap; her right arm was supported and loosely Velcro-strapped to the wheelchair's armrest.

Let's be honest—at this point, how many speakers and performers would probably have turned away and paid little or no attention to her, if not even outright ignored her as to not be "distracted" by seeing the difficult situation…and in the front row, no less? Many would probably seek out several friendly faces elsewhere in the crowd from whom to receive lively feedback during the show.

I did the exact opposite. I moved in even closer, determined to connect with her. As I approached, I smiled and said, "Thank you for coming to the program this evening." When I looked at her eyes through the dark sunglasses, I saw only an expressionless, blank stare; her eyes frozen. It was then that I realized this woman was unable to blink regularly, thus the protective sunglasses. Seated a few feet away and in the row behind her, a man called out to me, "She can't talk!" And, for a moment, neither could I.

"What is her name?" I asked him with a sense of quiet urgency. "Barbara," he replied. I didn't know how long this woman had been in such a deteriorating, medical condition and I didn't know how many more days she might have left. Not many, I'm guessing. Regardless, I wanted her to know that, on this night, I was validating her presence, acknowledging that she was still very much a living, human being. She was not just a nameless, faceless, lifeless body in a wheelchair. I put my hand on her right arm and quietly said, "Barbara, at the end of the show tonight, I'm going to sing a song for you. No one else—just you." She said nothing, nor did she move. She couldn't.

An hour and 15 minutes later, having playfully taken my audience on a joyful trip down comedy's Memory Lane, it was time to close the show. What no one knew—no one but me—was that I had never sang a song before in any of my shows. Sure, I'm an entertaining speaker, but I'm no Tony Bennett. What can I say? That moment when Barbara was brought into the room had so moved me that I felt this night had to be the night when I just stuck my neck out there and did something extra special and very personal for this woman.

The song I knew I had to sing in that moment was the song most often associated with Charlie Chaplin—Smile. He had written the music for it for his 1936 film, "Modern Times." But, there were no lyrics for the tune until 1954, when the songwriting team of Turner and Parsons submitted something that Chaplin would finally accept. That is why you will never find a recorded version of Smile with lyrics prior to 1954. Since then, many great recording artists have knocked out wonderful versions of the song. Not on that list, however, was me!

The moment had arrived. There was no turning back. True, the only person in the theater who even knew I had promised to sing a song was one woman, Barbara—and she couldn't talk. Had I closed out the show the way I normally do (with my poem, Lost and Found), no one would have ever known any differently.

Forgetting everyone else in the theater, my laser focus was now on one woman. I walked over to Barbara, knelt down on one knee and carefully put my left hand on her right hand, holding it gently. My right hand, remarkably steady considering the circumstances, held the microphone. Then, in a hushed tone filled with heartfelt emotion, I began to sing.

> Smile, though your heart is aching.
> Smile, even though it's breaking.
> When there are clouds in the sky,
> you'll get by.

If you smile through your fear and sorrow,
Smile – and maybe tomorrow,
You'll see the sun come shining through
for you.

Light up your face with gladness.
Hide every trace of sadness,
Although a tear may be ever so near.
That's the time you must keep on trying.
Smile – what's the use of crying.
You'll find that life is still worthwhile
If you just smile.

When I finished the song, the audience (whom I had forgotten even existed) applauded in unified, emotional approval. Slowly looking up, I noticed that the man who had earlier told me, "She can't talk," was sobbing uncontrollably and fumbling for his handkerchief to wipe his eyes and blow his nose.

I rose to my feet, leaned over Barbara, gave her a kiss on her right cheek and then spoke softly into her right ear, "I love you."

Had the story ended there, it would have been memorable enough. But, then came the singular moment of the entire night. It is also, to this day, one of the singular most powerful moments of my career. With what little breath Barbara could muster, she ever-so-faintly and slowly whispered into my right ear, "T-h-a-n-k Y-o-u."

I was stunned. Absolutely stunned. Wouldn't you be, too? Taking a moment to gather my wits about me, and also allowing the room to catch its breath, I then proceeded to share the following poem with the entire audience. It is a piece that I wrote a few years ago, specifically with my senior audiences in mind.

Lost and Found
You may lose your thinning hair,
And you may lose your hearing.
You may lose your teeth. And ladies,
You may lose an earring.

Laryngitis means you've lost your voice.
The blind have lost their sight.
Some find they see more clearly now,
Knowing everything's alright.

Sometimes you lose your train of thought.
You've tried to lose some weight.
People often lose their car keys.
Where they're going, they go late.

Anglers never lose the memory
Of that fish they almost caught.
Hotheads quickly lose their temper.
Self-control is all for naught.

You may lose your reputation –
Have your name dragged through the dirt.
Sometimes you lose a button
From your favorite denim shirt.

It hurts when people lose their job.
Even lawyers lose a case.
On TV in the 60's,
The Robinsons were "Lost in Space."

In winter, you may lose a glove.
Politicians lose elections.
Bad golfers tend to lose their balls.
Male lovers lose erections.

If you gamble drunk in Vegas,
You may bet (and lose) the house.
With long life, from time or illness,
You may one day lose a spouse.

Some seniors lose their license.
But, they haven't lost their drive.

Their wit is sharp, their mind alert.
They're very much alive.

Time has a way of changing us.
We sometimes lose our touch.
No longer sweat the little things.
They don't matter all that much.

When feeling low, when spirits sag,
Some lose the will to live.
With laughter, cope. Find faith. Find hope.
Find one more hug to give.
In life, we lose possessions.
But, other "gifts," we find.
To smile despite our challenges –
Yes, it's all a state of mind.

So, every day, the choice is yours –
Will you be a doom-and-gloomer?
Buck up old chum – don't be so glum.
Never lose your sense of humor.

- Lenny Dave

Dear reader, realizing that some of you are many years away from the senior audience I have described above, I would like to share some additional thoughts that I hope provide an uplifting message, an inspirational action statement, if you will.

Four Words Forward

Listen

Listen to your "voice." Listen carefully—it's there, amidst the quiet noise and deafening silence. Listen—it calls out only to you. Know who you are. Find your "voice"—start now—because the longer you wait, the less likely you are to find it at all.

Create

Creatively express yourself. Discover your "core genius." At what do you excel? Do it! Realize and manifest your creative talent, whether it be in the Arts, the Sciences, in Sport or in Business. You are the conduit—you are the channel—you and you alone.

Share

Share your "gift" with the world. With skill, use your hands. With knowledge, use your head. With compassion, use your heart. Let the world know you exist. Let the world know you were here. How sad it would be to take your divinely inspired "gift" to the grave without ever sharing it with others.

Inspire

Inspire those around you by your actions. The secret of getting ahead, is getting started! Take action—make something happen! People expect and appreciate boldness in their leaders—whether in a nation or a neighborhood. Inspire others by your actions, your integrity and your example.

Listen—Create—Share—Inspire. Four words to guide you, as forward you go.

In closing, dear reader, I offer this benediction, this blessing, as I wish you a life filled with contentment, happiness and peace.

> Find the strength that lifts your spirit
> in those moments of despair.
> Know you're loved by friends and family
> when it seems like none are there.
>
> For your precious gifts, be thankful
> as you wander through the haze.
> This, too, shall pass in time. And then,
> be blessed with brighter days.

- Lenny Dave

Takeaways

1. Pay attention to the world around you. It delivers meaningful messages regularly. Put down your cell phone. Look up. Wake up. Speak up. Take action. Make something positive happen.

2. People matter. And, even if it appears that "no one is home", remember that, inside, a person's pilot light is still on until it is completely extinguished.

3. Do not measure yourself against others and certainly not by comparing job titles and possessions. As Einstein once said, "Everybody is a genius. But, if you judge a fish by its ability to climb a tree, it will live its whole life believing that it is stupid."

2 The First Word
Barry Fidelman

My opening statement is, *You don't have to be a Rhodes Scholar to be right, but who in the world is going to listen to you?* Well, I have beaten those odds because, if you are reading this, you are listening! I have no college degree but am a student of human nature. I was raised in a strange environment in that my family owned and operated a predominantly Jewish resort in South Haven, Michigan. From an early age, I learned to solve guest and employee problems by watching experts such as my parents (Irving and Sheila Fidelman) who were master host and hostess.

My nature as a young man growing up was extremely competitive. I excelled in sports and couldn't stand the thought of losing any competition or debate I entered into. I lived with people who were also strong-willed and argumentative. Quite often, these disagreements would become violent and physical. Sibling fights were common with my brothers and verbal arguments common with my mother. Sheila was the kindest and most generous person I knew. She would do anything for anybody if it was within her power. Her one drawback was a bipolar personality and it was quite often violent. It is said that *It takes two to make an argument.* Well, that is not true. When Sheila was raging, no one said a word and it would build as each moment went on.

I was working in the resort kitchen during the evening dinner hour. Sheila walked in the dining room's swinging door with anger on her face and with her right hand, she spread a whole stack of aluminum serving trays on the floor. She looked over at me and as she went back into the dining room, she swung her head at me and clenched her teeth together with a fake smile and said, "Just smile and say sheeeeeet." She loved Joan Crawford and she was as fine an actress as Joan.

We lived with the Mommy Dearest method of raising children. One day, we were arguing in her bedroom. She had a large room with a complete wall of glass-mirrored closet doors. As we were arguing, she had her back to the closet and I was facing the mirrored wall. As I began to defend myself, I saw myself in the mirror and realized how ugly and contorted my face was as I said my first word of response. I suddenly calmed and thought about how I was going to get out of this situation and somehow, I had the wherewithal to think about what I had to do that day! I walked out with her still yelling at me and went to work.

This event happened so often that I was able to train myself to divert my thought process every time, and never say that all important *first word* of response to an argument. When arguing with someone and they lose control of their temper, they have invited you to join them on the floor in an all-out rumble. The first word of response you use will determine whether you stand tall and watch them or dive to the floor and join them. This technique is not easy to master when you do not get to practice it often. I got to practice it almost every day! Sheila never saw the irony of it when she called me "you little son of a bitch" all the time!

Irving was one of the smartest and most well-read people I knew. He was the fairest decision maker, always having the ability to put himself in the other guy's shoes. Irving was a world-class tenor who loved to perform for his guests. Singing the old tunes, Irving and Sheila performed a nightly duet. I used to joke with him that he was the most booked singer in Michigan, although he had to build his own place to do it! Before he would take the stage, he would have a cup of tea and return the cup to the cup rack in the dish room. I was a young man with my first job in the dish room. Another young man and I were washing dishes having fun throwing food at each other. We would duck and throw, laughing all the time. One time, he didn't duck and I hit him in the face. He was just staring at the front. Laughing, I looked around and saw Irving in his tux putting his cup in the rack. He looked at me with a disgusted look and said, "Well son, you only live once" and as I watched him walk away he muttered, "but you're not going to make it."

He was wrong, because here I am writing this chapter for this book!

As a young man, I once came home with some rednecked local youths that were using the N-word like water. After they left, my father sat me down and asked me if these were my good friends. I said, "No, Dad" but they had been threatening me and I thought if I buttered up to them, they would leave me alone. He looked me in the eye and said, "Barry, a man without enemies is a man without principle! You can't agree with everyone just to keep more friends. Let it be known what you stand for, and if you like yourself and what you have been taught, stay the course."

I have the pleasure of co-raising a daughter with one of the finest mothers in the world. My ex-wife is a fair but stern parent, and I am fair but laid-back and demand little of our daughter. Mary, on the other hand, is quite demanding and settles for nothing less than excellence from the people around her. Ana, our daughter, had learning problems throughout her early schooling. She could not read and comprehend at her age level so we sought help with this disability. Ana also used to get into arguments with her mother which sometimes became quite violent. She was diagnosed with Disruptive Mood Dysregulation Disorder. (DMDD is a condition of extreme irritability, anger, and frequent, intense temper outbursts.)

One day, I got a call from her mom saying that she was locked in her bedroom and Ana was outside the door, threatening her. I could hear Ana saying, "I don't care!" in the muffled background. I immediately went over and as I entered the front door, I saw Ana standing outside her mother's bedroom door saying, "I don't care!" over and over. Looking at her, I said, "Ana, what's the problem?" She responded, "I don't care!" She was "locked up" in a depressed state. In seeing that no response was forthcoming, I just turned to the front door and started talking to the door, "Ana is such a wonderful young lady, what do you think is wrong with her? Door, "She must be very upset about something or she wouldn't be acting like this." This conversation went on for about one minute and I finally heard Ana yell at me from the top of the stairs, "Dad, you are talking to the door!" I turned to her and said, "Yes, but at least I am having a conversation."

She broke out of her locked depression and started to talk to me. Our little girl is now 17 and is a good student who holds a steady job while going to school. She even has a boyfriend and both are model citizens. The lesson to be learned in this story is that when someone is locked up in a depressed state and it turns aggressive, doing something like talking to the door or any other diversion that is bizarre sometimes jolts them back to reality.

Being a student of human nature has always sparked my interest. I would observe and react to customer and employee needs on a daily basis. I always liked to talk and ask questions of unusual and happy couples. I was working the front desk one check-in day, looking forward to seeing families that have been coming to the resort for years and years.

One such family was Sam and Helen Cohen. They have packed their car and made the trip to South Haven for the last 40 years. The time in the car was probably the longest they have spent in one room together in the past year! Most people are irritable after the long ride and we at the desk have to mellow them out. Not so with Sam and Helen! They would walk in holding hands, smile and say, "Is our room ready?"

I finally just had to ask them, "What is the secret of your lengthy marriage and happiness?"

Sam smiled and said, "Mr. Fidelman, I attribute our success to holding hands!"

"But Sam, just holding hands made you both happy?"

"That's right. If I ever let go, I believe I will choke her to death!"

Well there you go folks—we all learn little tricks to help live our lives together more comfortably. It's our human nature!

Never be afraid to ask someone to explain what they mean when you do not understand their comment. Too often, we just let it go and get the wrong concept of their opinion. After the summer resort season, we would go to Canton, Ohio to my mom's home town. Grandma Coleman lived in a mixed neighborhood and their neighbors were named the Andolora's. I remember one day I was playing in the backyard while Grandma Coleman and Mrs. Andolora were hanging their laundry up to dry. They were talking over the fence and could barely see each other's face. Mrs. Andolora said in her Italian accent, "My daughter she hava tripletsa. That happens once ina one-hundred anda forty-thousand times!" Grandma Coleman responds, "Von hundred forty thousand times! Ven does she have time to do her houseverk?" She might better have asked what she meant before jumping to conclusions.

Celebrate your successes with little fanfare and spend as much time as necessary trying to analyze your defeats or mistakes. The one rule I have in analyzing mistakes or defeats is never point your finger at someone else, always point that finger at yourself and ask yourself *What could I have done differently?* If someone else doesn't do their job, ask yourself *What made me think he could or would do this job?* If you require this answer every time, you will be one smart person when you get to my age! Sometimes, we hire out of convenience or friendship which clouds the issue of getting the job done! There are two ways to handle mistakes: get depressed with yourself or get excited and see it as an opportunity to learn something new about your decision-making skills! Time to put on your big-boy pants and get smarter!

In summing up my small piece of literary history, I wish to leave you with these five points to ponder:

Takeaways

1. When dealing with someone who is angry and yelling at you, train yourself to divert your attention before responding with that first word out of your mouth. You have a choice of joining them rolling on the floor or remaining in that high place of self-esteem.

2. A man without enemies is a man without principle. Not all people should be your friends if they hold opposing values.

3. When someone with a bipolar disorder is in a snit, I have found that the best way to stop the tantrum is to divert their attention to other subjects or act bizarre.

4. If you don't fully understand what someone has told you, it is your obligation to ask them to explain themselves. Don't just let it go without a full understanding.

5. Celebrate your successes little and dwell on your defeats or mistakes a lot. Never point your finger at someone else, point it at yourself and ask What could I have done differently to change the outcome?

3 The Day I Met Santa
David Coleman

Like dozens of times before, I found myself racing through Atlanta's Hartsfield Airport like I was navigating an obstacle course. Hartsfield is the busiest airport in the world and I was darting in between people, luggage and golf carts like a rodeo clown escaping a mad bull. My flight had landed late, my next flight was leaving soon, and my departure gate could not have been farther away. If I somehow make my flight, I make my speaking appearance. If not, I miss it and the circus begins.

As I neared the gate, panting and bordering on complete exhaustion, I could see they were still boarding as the flight's departure had been delayed. Phew, I caught a break and felt a sense of relief. Maybe this day wouldn't be so bad after all.

As a high-mileage frequent flyer, I was able to board the moment I arrived. I walked down the long jetway, through the door, and onto the plane. After exchanging pleasantries with the flight crew, I passed through first class (which I was not fortunate enough to be enjoying this day). I was assigned to sit on the aisle in the second row of coach seating. As I passed the bulkhead wall, he immediately caught my eye. Santa! Santa Claus was on my flight and sitting right in front of me!

Now I am not talking about a rent-a-Santa like we see dressed up during the holidays. No, I was staring at *the real deal*. Old Kris Kringle himself, or at least a dead ringer doppelganger for him. Santa was sitting in the front row of coach right on the aisle. He had obviously boarded early and had his eyes closed, was covered in the complimentary blanket they provide and enjoying the small, square white pillow nestled behind his head.

He was not in costume, but Santa had it all. A dense, thick white beard. Long, flowing, curly white hair. Thick white eyebrows. I figured he had worked hard over the holidays and was on his way to vacation—somewhere tropical, I would imagine.

I settled in behind him and watched as the plane continued to board. The final three people to board the flight were a mother (in her 30's) and two small children (who appeared to be twins). They were dressed alike and simply adorable. The mother pinned the boy against the window (smart move), put herself in the middle and placed her daughter on the aisle across from Santa. This mother had traveled before.

As the minutes passed by, the plane became hotter and stuffier as there was very little air passing through the vents and it was a blisteringly hot day in Atlanta. As the temperature rose, the children began to fidget as their mother did her best to keep them comforted and entertained. At that moment, Santa began to stir. He looked over at the little girl and said, "Honey, you're hot, aren't you?" She said, "Yes, I am." He said, "Well then, would you like a fan?" The little girl perked up and said, "Yes, I'd love a fan!" At that moment, Santa reached over and pulled out a sack. The man had a sack! He put his hand inside and pulled out a relatively small piece of what appeared to be black plastic. I remember thinking to myself, "Santa, that is not a fan, you're high and you're disappointing a child!" To my surprise, he unsnapped the plastic, pulled it apart and snapped it back together again and, in doing so, transformed it into a pleated Japanese plum fan. It was colorful, functional and made the young girl incredibly happy. She began to giggle, fan Santa, fan her mother, fan her brother, fan me, fan the wall, fan the vent, she fanned everyone and everything she could find. She was ecstatic.

Seeing his sister so happy, the little boy erupted. "I want a fan. I want a fan too!" "Of course, you do", replied Santa. He reached back into the sack (the man had a sack!) and pulled out one of those small, battery-operated, handheld fans with three flexible, plastic, non-threatening blades. He handed the fan to the boy's mother, she turned it on, fanned herself for a moment and handed it to her son. He immediately went to fan heaven. He fanned himself, his mother, the window—you get the picture.

Seeing both of her children elated and positively distracted, the mother looked over at Santa, smiled, nodded and sighed. Translated, I believe this meant, *God bless your soul*, in mother, to Santa. I took the opportunity to tap Santa on his outside shoulder. He turned his head toward me and I said, "Way to go, Santa." He was a good sport and replied, "Ho, ho, ho, son. Ho, Ho, Ho." Then, I left him alone to his relaxation and plane ride.

An important lesson learned

As the plane took off, we all settled in. Atlanta to Salt Lake City takes several hours to complete and the whoosh of the engines and air stream knocked many people out, including me. Seemingly minutes later, the wheels hitting the ground in Utah woke us all back up.

When commercial jets land, the passengers immediately begin to jockey for position to deplane as quickly as possible. I remember thinking, *Santa is a big guy and may have luggage. If I don't block traffic a bit and help him, he could be sitting on this plane for quite a while.* So, that is exactly what I did. I slowly retrieved my carry-ons, put on my sport coat and began to block traffic. A line formed behind me and I could sense laser beams of discontentment being shot directly through my back.

I leaned forward and said to Santa, "Sir, go ahead, grab your stuff and get off the plane. I am holding people up for you." He said, "Son, that is very kind of you, but I can't" and he pulled away his blanket. It was only then that I noticed that he was a double amputee, having had both legs amputated just above the knee. My heart sank.

I stepped in front of him (as the glaring throng passed by) and said, "Sir, I am so incredibly sorry to have embarrassed you in any way. I was just trying to be helpful. You and I have bonded a bit on this flight. Do you mind if I ask you what happened?" He said, "No, I don't mind" and went on to explain. "On our 40th wedding anniversary, my wife and I were headed out to our favorite restaurant. We were hit head-on by a drunk driver. She was killed instantly and I was pinned in such a way that it resulted in me having done what you see here today."

"Where are you headed?" I asked. He said, "I am headed to the west coast to see my grandson. He was born prior to the accident and I have never seen him in person." I said to him, "Sir, you are remarkable, and I am just not sure I could be where you are today. You lost your wife in a tragic way. You lost the use of your legs in a horrific way, yet, here you are traveling alone and even helping others on the plane as you do. I am not sure I could be as strong, nor as compassionate as you have been through what you have experienced." His response changed my life and I hope it impacts yours as well. He said, "Son, did I make those children happy? Did I put a smile on their face? Did I ease that mother's burden? Did I make them laugh? Did I make you laugh?" I said, "Yes, to all those things." He said, "Then I paid honor to my wife, because she now lives in my heart and when I do things for others or make people laugh, I pay honor to her."

I was stunned and at that moment, I realized that I had learned five very important things:

1. We choose our attitude every single day.
2. I needed to quit whining about things in life that truly did not matter.
3. I had just met an incredible man with a remarkably positive attitude and outlook on life.
4. I needed to share his message with as many people as possible.
5. I learned that life itself writes our best material if we are simply smart enough to open our eyes, ears, and hearts and learn from the interactions we encounter every day.

Thus, I have shared Santa with you.

On a daily basis, I now find myself asking, "What would Santa do?" if he found himself in my position. For example, if I am facing a horribly difficult week of travel and appearances that seems overwhelming, I ask myself "What would Santa do?" The answer: He would take a long, hard look at the week's schedule, form a plan of action to meet all goals and exceed all expectations, eat well, exercise, stay connected to family and friends, revel in the company of others, and learn from every person and every interaction to make himself a better person.

To me, Santa is a mindset whereby your first thought every day should be, *Today is potentially the best day of my life! How do I live it to the best of my ability in order to have the greatest impact on others?* From this day forward, I ask you to do the same. Instead of whining or complaining when you face a challenge or when you receive less than favorable news or results, ask yourself, "What would Santa do?" and live that moment with purpose and intention. Let Santa be your motivation and guide to living a more fulfilling, intentional life with no regrets.

Was my father Santa-like?

As I wrote this chapter, I realized that I just might have been lucky enough to grow up with Santa as a father. I realized that my father, Marvin, taught me many lessons about life, love and leadership if I was simply smart enough to pause, reflect upon them, incorporate them into my life and pass them on to others.

One particular example quickly came to mind. I was a freshman in college at Bowling Green State University. Having grown up with a father who was a professional gambler, I knew a lot more about certain things, like playing poker, than any of my friends. I had a group of close friends that loved to play cards and we played often. We didn't have a ton of money (what struggling college student does?) so we used our meal coupon books as currency. Back then, we did not have a scan card with a magnetic strip that carried all of our cash or tracked our transactions. We had coupon books, comprised of $250 in currency per book, broken down into denominations of $.25, $.50, $1.00, and $5.00 serrated coupons. This made playing poker quite easy as it was just like having actual money at our disposal.

Due to my background, I was a much better player than my friends and I often won, a lot. One particular Friday night, we were playing and my father surprised me by visiting unannounced. Although it was great to see him, I was doing quite well in this game and had accumulated most of my friend's "money." I was on a roll and wanted to finish what I started.

Seeing this, and without letting me know, my father asked me to run down the street and get a few things for him while he took my place and played for a while. I remember him saying, "Guys, this looks like fun. You won't take advantage of an old man if I play a bit, will you?" My friends all said, "Of course not, Mr. Coleman, sit right down." My dad was friendly, charismatic, humorous and my friends loved him. Everyone did. There was nothing not to love.

It took me about 30 minutes or more to run the errands my father asked me to complete. When I returned, I was shocked and angered to see that he had lost back nearly all the "money" I had accumulated before I walked away to run his errands. Interestingly enough, it looked as if the money had been equally distributed around the table. He appeared to have lost at least one big hand to every one of my friends. Furious, I asked my father if he could join me in my room for a moment. As we entered, I unleashed on him and let him have it. I spewed venom. "How could you lose all my money back? You are a much better player than that, what is wrong with you? Are you trying to lose on purpose just to hurt me?" I went far beyond that for quite a while, I am sure, yet he did not retaliate in kind.

What my father said next changed my life forever. He said, "Davey (his nickname for me), you grew up differently than these kids. You have been playing poker since you were a young boy and are a much better player than they are. It is wrong for you to take all their money, especially the food coupons they need to eat. If and when you need money, you can always call your mother and I and if we can help, we will, but I do not want to hear about you taking money from your friends like this again. *The next time I hear you talk about time spent with your friends, I want to hear words like joy and laughter, not heartache and pain.*"

His words went through me like a dagger. In his Santa-like way, my father had taught me not to use any of my God-given or learned talents to the detriment of others and that time spent with my friends was important and precious.

Santa taught me that we choose our attitude every single day and no matter our personal circumstance, we can still be of service to others. My father taught me that time spent with others is precious and that our talents should be used for good, not evil.

Are there *Santa-like* moments in your life that you can reflect upon? Lessons you can learn and share if you will only stop to reflect upon them? My guess is yes, dozens of them. The question is, will you take the time necessary to reflect upon what has brought you to this point in your life and live with purpose and intention? Will you treat tomorrow as potentially the greatest day of your life, set goals, form a plan of action and revel in your interactions with others? Only you know the answer. As you think back on this chapter, please remember a few takeaways:

Takeaways

1. We choose our attitude every single day.

2. No matter what personal circumstances we find ourselves facing, we can still be of service to others and be a force for good in the world.

3. Live a purpose-driven life full of good intentions and watch how this reflects back on you. What we project to the world, comes back tenfold.

4. We should always use our God-given, natural or learned skills, abilities, and talents for the betterment of others.

5. When facing an obstacle, ask yourself, "What would Santa do?" and while you are at it, throw in there, "What would Marvin do?

4 Mental Health & Other Myths
Sherry McCamley

My earliest childhood memory is from when I was three or four years old. I was awakened in the middle of the night by yelling and loud banging noises. I ran from my bed to see my mother, lying on the floor in the hallway, with my father standing over her, beating her with a loaf of bread. In retrospect, it almost seems funny; I mean, what kind of damage can you do with a loaf of soft Wonder Bread? But as you can imagine, it was a terrifying sight for a small child to witness. Although I couldn't know or understand it then, this was my introduction to alcoholism, mental illness, and a dysfunctional family life.

Unfortunately, the episode with the bread was not an isolated incident. I spent most of my childhood and teenage years living in fear and watching the clock. I knew if it hit 7 pm and my father wasn't home from work yet, he had probably stopped at a bar for drinks, and we were likely in for a long night of drunken verbal and physical abuse. I hated the feeling of not having any control over my situation and being afraid all the time. So, although I don't remember this as a conscious choice, early on, I chose anger over fear. Many years ago, a therapist told me that when in crisis, we often respond with either anger/fight or fear/flight. Anger is a powerful emotion, while fear is a powerless emotion. Being the oldest child, I was the one stepping in the middle of the fights, pulling my Dad off my mother and fighting back as much as I could.

Because of the stigma and shame surrounding addiction and mental illness, families often work very hard to keep others from finding out the terrible secret. Growing up, I never told any of my friends or teachers about my home life. My Dad was always able to work and keep a job, and he could be quite charming, so from the outside, it looked like we had a fine life. It was bad enough our family life was such a mess, I wasn't going to add to the damage by telling people about it. But, after a particularly bad battle at home one night when I was in high school, I decided to tell my boyfriend what was going on. After years of keeping the anger, frustration, and fear bottled up inside, the words just poured out. I realized later that I had taken quite a risk—after hearing about my crazy family, my boyfriend might have run for the hills! But, that decision to let someone in, to loosen the hold that stigma had on me, was the beginning of the healing process for me.

Years later, I was married to the boyfriend I confided in (he was a good listener!) and thinking about having children of my own. I was determined that my children would have a much better, less challenging childhood than I had. However, some issues and patterns from my childhood had followed me into my adult life. That anger that helped me cope as a child was now my go-to response in most situations. Whenever I felt my sense of "being in control" was threatened or challenged—which happens often to someone who is early in their marriage and career—I got mad and yelled and let everyone know I was mad. I just figured that was part of my personality—I had a bad temper. But being a mom with a bad temper would be in direct conflict with my goal to provide a much better childhood for my kids. Thus began a journey of many years into learning and self-discovery.

You know the saying "You can choose your friends but you can't choose your family." I did not choose to grow up in a dysfunctional family situation, but it appeared it was still having a major impact on me even though I hadn't lived with my family in years. I realized I needed to figure out what was going on and what to do about it. My first therapist pointed out the anger=power connection I had made as a child. This coping mechanism that served me well as a child was now counterproductive. Even though I was no longer under constant threat, I still reacted like I was. My therapist suggested support groups like Adult Children of Alcoholics, where I learned that behaviors I thought were just aspects of my personality were actually a response to being impacted by someone with an addiction.

At first, I was very frustrated by this. It was good to know it wasn't just me, or my flaws, that were causing issues. But, I didn't choose to grow up in a dysfunctional household, and yet I was still suffering from the effects of someone else's addiction and mental illness. Slowly, over time and through a lot of hard work, I made a very important discovery. I could not do anything about the past, but I could make my own decisions about the present and the future. And this is what I decided:

I will not be defined and controlled by my past. I will choose my path.

Sounds great, right? Well, I found out this is easier said than done. This decision meant I had to do a lot more work on myself. Many more hours and months and years of self-education and self-reflection were required. This problem had started with my Dad. Was he just a bad, evil person? Or, at a minimum, severely flawed? Several years after I moved out, my father stopped drinking. And yet, many of the issues we had attributed to drinking remained. Eventually, he was hospitalized and diagnosed with depression. I didn't know much about depression, or mental illness in general, so I started asking a lot of questions and reading everything I could on the topic. Here are things I didn't know, and you might not know either:

One in four adults in the US experience mental illness in a given year—62 million Americans.

Fifty percent of people with a mental illness also have an addiction of some kind.

Mental illness was much more common than I thought, and there was clearly a link between mental illness and addiction. My therapist explained that people with an undiagnosed mental illness often self-medicate with alcohol and/or drugs to try to mask and manage their symptoms. So, my Dad wasn't bad or evil or flawed, he was ill. Realizing he was ill, not evil, started me down the path of forgiveness, which also helped my healing process.

Mental illness

There is a strong genetic component to mental illness and mental health issues. After my father was hospitalized, my mother reached out to his brothers to let them know. She found out that all three of his brothers had also been hospitalized for depression, but no one talked about it because of the stigma! Your family may have a history of mental illness, but if you never talk about it like in my family, or if you mistake the addiction for the whole story, you may not know.

Since one of the things that can determine if you are predisposed to a mental illness is whether or not you have a family history of it, this new information about my family tree got my attention. I began watching for signs of depression in myself and my actions and, sure enough, I was diagnosed with depression as well. My sister also has been diagnosed with depression, and our brother has bipolar disorder.

It is interesting to me how often we resort to labels when talking about mental illness and mental health issues. You often hear people say, "She's crazy!" or "He's nuts!" or "That person is mentally ill." Do we say, "She's cancer" or "He's heart disease" or "That person is Alzheimer's?" No, we say, "She has cancer" or "He suffers from heart disease." No wonder people with mental illness tend to define themselves by their illness, the rest of us do it with our language. Realizing this, I made another decision:

I will not be defined and controlled by my mental illness.

Because I am willing to talk about my mental health issues and mental illness, I have had quite a few one-on-one conversations with people who then share their stories. And everyone has a story about mental illness. NAMI, National Alliance on Mental Illness, notes that:

Everyone has a family member, co-worker, or friend that is affected by mental illness.

One theme that consistently comes up in these conversations, centers around attitude. Since mental illness involves the mind, many people seem to think that "it's all in your head" or "mind over matter" can be applied. Like those Facebook memes imply— "You're only as happy as you make up your mind to be"—some think that mental illness is a sign of weakness or lack of willpower. Say a guy has a broken leg. We know he's injured because he's hobbling around with a cast and crutches. Would we say to that guy, "Hey! It's all in your leg. If you try hard enough you can throw those crutches away and still run that marathon!" We wouldn't say that, right? So why do we say things like that to the mentally ill?

This distinction between mental illness and physical illness makes no sense to me. Someone with a mental illness is just as injured as the person with a broken leg. Mental illness is a biological brain disorder;

there's just no cast or scar to make it visible. Mental illness is not a matter of a character flaw, or a person not trying hard enough.

Addiction

Speaking of character flaws, do you think addiction is a character flaw? Are addicts weak or lazy people with no self-control? I used to think that way about addicts and addiction too. The American Medical Association and the American Public Health Association both have defined addiction as a disease for many years. And today, with advances in DNA research and brain imaging, we know so much more about the brain and addiction.

Roughly ten percent of the population is genetically predisposed to addiction.

Studies have shown that roughly ten percent of the population is genetically predisposed to addiction. Have you ever wondered why it is that so many people experiment with and use alcohol and drugs, but only some become addicted? It is because one in ten of us has an addict gene in our DNA. Having the addict gene is not destiny. Some people with the gene do not become addicted, and people without the gene can become addicted if they abuse alcohol and drugs. But, a person with the addict gene who tries smoking, or alcohol or drugs is much more likely to become addicted than someone who does not have the addict gene.

Forty million Americans age 12 and over meet the clinical criteria for addiction involving nicotine, alcohol or other drugs.

This is according to a Columbia University study. That's more Americans than those with heart disease, diabetes or cancer. The National Institute on Drug Abuse says, "Addiction occurs when a person cannot control the impulse to use drugs even when there are negative consequences. These behavioral changes are also accompanied by changes in brain functioning, especially in the brain's natural inhibition and reward centers…. Brain imaging studies from people addicted to drugs show physical changes in areas of the brain that are critical for judgment, decision-making, learning, memory, and behavior control." So, addiction is much more about brain chemistry and genetics than character flaws. It is a physical, biological condition, and the sooner we start treating it as such, the sooner we can reach actual solutions.

With what I know now about mental illness and addiction, I have much more compassion for my father and a better understanding of why things were the way they were in my household growing up, although I don't condone or excuse his behavior. I have shared this journey of realization and healing with many people over the years in private conversations. One such conversation a few years ago led to a real breakthrough.

What can I do?

I am a singer, songwriter, actor, piano player, director, and teacher, and have been for many years. As a creative person involved in the arts, I often work collaboratively with other artists on projects. While producing a show with an actor/director friend of mine, Cathy Springfield, we talked about our families and experiences growing up, and realized we had both been affected by mental illness and addiction. Both of us also deal with mental illness of our own, my depression and Cathy's bipolar disorder. We discussed the daunting issues we had encountered: the "conspiracy of silence" where people don't talk openly about mental illness, the stigma, the lack of awareness and compassion. We talked about the frustration of only being one person trying to combat these issues, and in a moment of true, creative inspiration we said, "We should write a show about mental illness!" And, over the next 2 years, that is exactly what we did.

Not just any show, mind you. Cathy is funny, and I am a musician, so this would not be some heavy drama or dry lecture. Our show would educate and entertain with songs and humor. But we felt it was critical to tell our own stories openly and honestly, not create made-up characters. If we wanted people to talk about mental illness, we would start with ourselves. We also asked my daughter, Erin, to share her stories about mental health issues. Our show, "She's Crazy: Mental Health and Other Myths," has been described as "an interactive, entertaining cabaret show that educates, uplifts, and inspires audiences." We wrote the show with the goal of increasing awareness about mental health issues and reducing the stigma surrounding mental illness. Now we can reach many more people.

After every performance, audience members come up to us and share their stories about their challenges, and concerns about loved ones, and hopes and fears about the future.

My journey of realization and healing continues. I followed a process that allowed me to get help for my challenges and ultimately help others at the same time. Whatever your challenge, if you want to help yourself and others, you can try this process too:

Talk about it

When confronting a major life challenge, we often feel isolated and alone, and that we have to address the issue by ourselves. Talk therapy, group therapy, and support groups are all effective for many people because expressing our thoughts, feelings, and fears and hearing others do the same can be very helpful. But, even if you aren't comfortable with any of those approaches, find someone you can talk to. Being willing to talk and share will help you begin to define the issues and what to do about them.

Learn about it

It's not like I enjoy doing research. But, I have gotten so much comfort from knowing that it is not just me; 62 million other people also experience mental illness, everyone is affected by it, brain chemistry and genetics play a major role, and addiction is a disease. This knowledge helps me be much more compassionate about my family history, about fellow sufferers, and most importantly, toward myself. Knowledge is power— learn as much as you can about whatever life challenge you are dealing with.

Collaborate—ask for help

I decided long ago that whatever embarrassment I might feel about sharing my problems was outweighed by the help I could get. I know I certainly don't have all the answers, and the only way I get them from others is to ask. Joining hands and minds with Cathy and Erin allowed us to do something I could not have done alone—write a show! Think about who you can work with to help you do the heavy lifting.

Bring your unique gifts and strengths_

Each of us is unique, with our own set of gifts and strengths and weaknesses. Our challenges are likely not unique, but our response certainly can be. It is not unique that I had a dysfunctional childhood, or was impacted by addiction, or have mental health issues. But how many people with those challenges write and perform in a cabaret show about them? I responded in a way that is very connected to who I am and what I do. What unique gifts and strengths can you bring to bear on your challenges?

Takeaways

1. Learn about mental illness and addiction, and the causes and impact of each.

2. Have more compassion for people who deal with mental illness and addiction.

3. Learn about a process to get help for challenges and help others at the same time: talk about it, learn about it, collaborate and ask for help.

4. Think about what unique gifts and strengths you can bring to bear to address life's challenges.

5. Talk about life's challenges and reduce the stigma surrounding them.

5 Is What You Thought You Heard, What I Thought I Said?

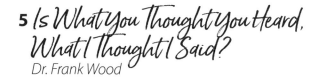

Dr. Frank Wood

*The single biggest problem in communication
is the illusion that it has taken place.*
-George Bernard Shaw

Let's be honest, communication can be challenging!

In this chapter, I share some thoughts on communication through a personal story about pizza (really the story is about communication).

After the story, I will share an idea that might help you with your ability to communicate more clearly, especially with people I call *important people*. In my pizza story, my *important people* are my daughter and me.

Your *important people*
Before you read on, consider your *important people*: a roommate, co-worker, child, mom or dad, brother, or that friend who you have not spoken with in years. As I share my story about *getting pizza*, my hope is that you will realize a similar story in your own life too, with your *important people*. This chapter is written for you. Are you the target audience for this chapter?

Businesspeople: Are you a sales professional who struggles with cold calls or the middle manager with a direct report?
Athletes: Are you a student athlete managing the demands of sport and school?
Parents or grandparents: Are you the parent or grandparent of a teenager with challenges?
High school or college students: Are you a college student who has a challenging class or a roommate who challenges you?

Ok, let's be honest. This chapter is written for anyone with *important people* relationships.

Communication Problem: The gap

In your *important people* conversations, you may have had the experience of speaking with that person and you thought you were completely clear about what you said, but they did not understand a word. Most of us have said to another person, "How many times do I need to tell you…? Finish your homework says the parent, *complete the task* says the boss, or *run the laps* says the coach. When this happens, there is a gap between what we *thought* we said and what the other person *thought* they heard.

My pizza story and my gap

This is a story about parenting, pizza, and that *gap*. A few years back, on a late afternoon in May, my 13-year-old daughter asked me to take her to dinner. Those of you who have ever had a 13-year-old daughter know that this is the parenting equivalent of seeing Bigfoot riding a jet ski. So off we went to grab a pizza. It was a popular neighborhood spot and a beautiful night, so when we arrived, there was a wait. I dropped my daughter off and told her I'd go park the car.

I parked, walked in, inhaled the pizza fumes and realized how hungry I actually was. My daughter said it was a 15-minute wait, as I'd expected. I found myself a sturdy wall to lean against while she pulled out her phone and did whatever it is 13-year-olds do with the most advanced technology mankind has ever known. 15 minutes passed. 20 minutes passed. 22.5 minutes passed. I asked my daughter if she was sure that it was only a 15-minute wait. She said yes. I checked with the hostess to see how much longer it would be. She scanned the list, reached the end, and told me that our names were not on it. Hmm.

I asked my daughter if she put our names on the list. She said no. She then mentioned that she'd learned about the wait time after hearing a family talk about *their* wait time. This could only mean one thing: she never gave our name to the receptionist at the popular pizzeria. Hmm.

At this point, I was no longer feeling that sense of excitement about pizza as it was replaced with tenseness akin to a Mount St. Helens volcanic eruption circa 1980 (well not really, but you get the point). I couldn't begin to fathom a valid reason she wouldn't put our names on the list and what rubbed sand into the proverbial wound was she showed zero remorse for her forgetfulness. As my mind filled with a portion of rage, I began peppering her with questions about why she didn't give our name to the hostess. Confused, she told me I never asked her to do that.

Reread that last part: I presumed she knew something that I did not tell her.

I exploded (technically, I imploded), and we left the restaurant. Not completely lost in my frustration, I did place a second order of pizza at a sister restaurant and as we drove from Pizzeria #1 to Pizzeria #2, I continued my inquisition of my daughter and her apparent lack of capacity to understand simple non-verbalized directives.

As I began to sputter, my voice raised a bit at my daughter for not being more like me. I did this fully aware that my daughter is not me and I am older than 13. Really mature, I know.

Now, for those who are reading and casting judgment and deeming yourselves so much more mature than I, I ask you to recall your last episode of "sputter".

I went from a place of calm, happy, and excited to a place where I was petty, impatient, frustrated, and angry in approximately 37/100ths of a second and I hate to break it to you, but I'm not alone in taking that path— we've all been there. Maybe it was this afternoon or yesterday morning or when you last spent time with your in-laws.

Did you know that there is science to what happened between my daughter and me?

The Polyvagal Theory

I hate it when my hopes for a great dinner with my daughter end in my engaging in a sputter. Let's be honest, doesn't that frost your Wheaties when you sputter with your *important people*? So, I introduce you to Stephen Porges, a scientist whose research intersects psychology, neuroscience, and evolutionary biology.

Stephen came up with a theory called the Polyvagal Theory, which involves how our nervous system controls our reactions and behaviors when life is challenging, demanding or stressful. I am not going to describe his theory in detail, but I will share an analogy that will help makes sense of this theory as it applies to our ability to communicate for impact.

When struggle meets understanding

I don't know about you but I struggle with how easily I move from *ok* to *sputter*. This Polyvagal Theory helps make sense of why each of us takes that path from *ok* to where we are not able to act like our brains are working. And yet, my friend Stephen has told me that all of the ways we take in and consider our experiences start out as adaptive or helpful. Let me say that in different words: *our brain is trying to help us, even when we are sputtering.*

Let's look at the pizza meal or ordeal, again.

On the day before my blood began to boil, my expectations for a great time led me to a state of excitement and so my heart was racing with positive hopes and expectations. Yet, after I began speaking, I noticed my heart racing and my stomach churning in response to my daughter's actions. I immediately focused on what I did NOT want—I left my hopes for a good meal to my being critical and negative. Has that ever happened to you? (Maybe just this week?)

When we lose it, we've lost it

The first thing I want to put on the table is that my reactions in life to my *important people* relate to my own (for you, *your* own) reactive neurophysiology. Our neurophysiology is how our body becomes activated in the face of challenges, demands, and threats. Our brain makes us think and act as if these challenges, demands, and threats (stressful stuff) are real and are happening right now! We get hijacked by this force that makes us take a READY—AIM—FIRE approach to solving the problem. Let's be honest, that is what I did on that day with my daughter. What is really sad is that I got so caught up in what I wanted, I lost my ability to be fully open to the reality of the situation.

Evolutionary survival

If we think about living in the Stone Age, the most important thing was to survive and reproduce. As we humans evolved, we developed ways to defend ourselves from external threats (like saber-toothed tigers). You may have heard of the fight-or-flight responses that evolved to deal with these predators. We see the tiger and we either stay and battle (fight response) or we run (flight response).

> The decision to battle or run is one our brain makes. When we think we can win a battle, **we stay to battle** (fight) and when we think the predator might win the battle, **we run** (flight).

Over time, our brain began to make that decision. Our brain evolved to help keep us safe. This evolution also permits our brain to move from REAL danger (a tiger chasing us) to IMAGINED danger (like the fear of a slamming door, or emotions we experience during a movie about Luke Skywalker). Internally, the processes are the same.

Polyvagal Theory (the science part)

According to the Polyvagal Theory, our brain and our "wiring" (our nerves) play an important role in how we respond to conversations or interactions that our brain determines are:

Safe: When we get a response we like—**we engage**.
Dangerous: When we get a response we don't like but our brain thinks we can do something about the issue—we **act**.
Life-threatening: When we get a response we don't like and it is overwhelming—**we freeze up**.

In a way, our brain responds to the data it takes in a lot like a computer and then decides—are things safe or not? An analogy, a comparison between two things, might help us understand the theory.

The analogy I will use is a traffic light. I use this analogy so much I created a logo for my speaking business. Let's consider how traffic lights work and how we work with traffic lights. When we see a **GREEN** traffic light we GO. When we see a **RED** traffic light, we STOP. Then there is the **YELLOW** light—well, that light is personal, from person-to-person and situation-to-situation. If you are running late for an important meeting, you might hit the gas pedal and speed through the intersection. If, however, a large truck is turning in front of you or you see a police officer, you might hit your brake pedal.

Green Light

How does this comparison help us understand why we sputter with our *important people*? Connect this analogy of the traffic light to our ability to communicate for impact. At green lights, we go. In communication, this is when we speak and listen for impact. Back to your brain and its wiring: when your brain thinks things are safe—all is deemed to be okay—this is when you speak and listen.

> With Green lights, there is a sense of calm and this is when we listen! Here, we engage.

On the way to the pizzeria, my daughter and I were filled with a sense of calm. In this moment, each of us spoke and listened with ease. In a past conversation you've had with one of your *important people*, you may remember a time where communication flowed easily. This is when each person is both listening and speaking with clarity.

Yellow Light

At yellow lights, we rattle; we do the fight-or-flight thing. In communication, this is when we over-talk, force our opinion, talk without listening and when listening, we finish the speaker's sentences, make assumptions, and become defensive.

Back to the pizzeria. This is when I approached the counter to ask about our table. I approached my daughter and I engaged in my sputter. I even had that voice inside my head telling me to tone it down. I did not listen. Ugh, this is where my yellow light can get me into trouble! Note: This yellow light experience can be helpful and at other times it can be destructive!

> With yellow lights, there is agitationand this is when we do not listen! Here, we act (fight-or-flight).

Red Light

At red lights, we stop. In communication, this is when we freeze up, go "deer in the headlights" and the words get stuck in our brain. What comes out of our mouth is not what we needed to say in that moment. Back to your brain and its wiring. When I went yellow light, my daughter almost immediately went to red light. She became very quiet. In a way, her brain was likely thinking things were dangerous. She may have thought, *this is too much*! She experienced a freeze response.

> At red lights, we are overwhelmed and this is when we are not listening. We hope the storm will end. (We freeze up.)

In closing

I hope you realize that when you are in a conversation, especially with your *important people*, you might consider how your brain is involved in your ability to communicate for impact and listen for clarity.

Just last week, I shared a pizza with my daughter with no sputter and she said to me, as we were both reaching for that last slice of pizza, "You know what I thought I said dad? I want the last slice!" We both smiled!

Takeaways

1. Your ability to communicate is influenced by your biology—your brain is hard-wired to seek safety. When things are deemed safe, we are getting a response we like. This is when we listen and speak with ease—we engage.

2. When things are deemed dangerous and we don't like what is happening—but our brain thinks we can do something about the issue—we do our fight-or-flight thing. We take action.

3. When things are deemed life-threatening and we don't like what is happening—and what is happening is overwhelming—we freeze up.

4. Paying attention is important. When I notice that I am sputtering or freezing up, I make the conversation safer—by the tone of my voice, my volume level, or putting a smile on my face. You know how to do this! When the other person is sputtering or freezing up, make the conversation safer. A person who feels safe in a conversation also feels heard.

5. Periodically, ask the other person, "Is what you thought you heard what I thought I said?" Be open to the fact that you might want to think about what you are saying before you say it. Attempt to be interested in the other person hearing what you are saying by confirming that what they thought they heard was actually what you thought you said. Do not presume that people can read your mind or know what you never told them!

6 There but for the Grace of God go I
Eve Shapiro

The first time I saw it, I thought it was an anomaly. Matthew was ahead of me in the grocery aisle. He was much younger then, cute as a button, the center of attention wherever he went, the life of the party, absolutely loved by all.

He was the most outgoing kid you'd ever see. He never met a person he couldn't talk to, even when he was pre-school age. He was someone who, once you'd met him, you'd never forget. I remember taking him to a Baltimore Orioles baseball game when he was about 6. We sat in the last row of the section and he basically held court with all the other adults who sat in that area discussing stats for all of the players and the outlook for the team. Years later, at a Washington Redskins game, one of those folks sat next to him at FedEx Field, remembered him, and the next thing I knew they had basically started up where they finished years earlier, only this time discussing football instead of baseball stats.

We always see folks when we are out and about who come up and start a conversation, calling Matthew by name, discussing events from the past. Events that for most of us would have been long forgotten, but because Matthew was part of the mix that day, the memory is still strong for those who were with him.

There is an old saying:

It takes a minute to find a special person
An hour to appreciate them
A day to love them
But then an entire lifetime to forget them

Matthew is one of these people.

As the years have passed, he's now 26, I have come to understand that what I saw when he was a child is a circumstance that will follow him forever. Unlike what I witnessed at the ballpark, reactions are sometimes unjustified and uncalled-for, almost demeaning. I have seen it numerous times and each time it takes every ounce of my being not to stop the person right there and give them a piece of my mind.

You see, Matthew is a young man who was born with cerebral palsy. Since a very early age, he has used a wheelchair to get around. Nothing about him is any different from any other person his age other than the fact that his legs don't work. He has the same likes and dislikes, the same aspirations to land that great job or do that great thing. In other words, he has the same prospects for the future as any other young adult who has not solidified their "next adventure."

In the grocery store that day I noticed a look that I have come to refer to as *the there but for the grace of God, go I* look. Not quite a grimace but very close to it. It is a visual, not verbal, expression of "Whew, I am so glad that is not a part of my life." It says, "I'm so lucky that I don't have to deal with something like that." It is an act of denial that we all have in us—that internal choice not to want to even think about the possibility that we are not invincible or that vulnerability exists within us all. It is a lie that we perpetuate to feel satisfied or fulfilled with the gifts that we have been given in life.

What that individual expresses when they walk by Matthew is the undeniable misunderstanding that Matthew's life is less fulfilled than others who are seen as "normal". That person does not see an individual who was very active in high school. They assume he spent his school days in that classroom down the hall, not participating in the student government as freshman class president. They assume he had limited writing skills, not that he was editor in chief of his school newspaper for two years. They think he got a "special" diploma at graduation, not that he was an honor student or that he was given one of the ten top awards bestowed upon graduating seniors by the school faculty. He was not honored because he was disabled but because he was Matthew, an outstanding, involved student who everybody knew and loved.

That person assumes Matthew is a liability to society, not an active member who is an asset. They fail to acknowledge the fact that he'd be able to work doing something more productive than tasks that you see individuals doing in sheltered workshops. They'd be shocked to learn that he has worked not only in the United States Department of Transportation but also in the Obama White House. Their image of how he spends his day is that he sits in front of a television playing video games from dawn to dusk, not that he is running his own disability consulting business where he tries to challenge all the perceptions and views I've listed above. Their view lacks any level of positivity because they see Matthew as broken.

MATTHEW IS NOT BROKEN, HE IS DIFFERENT. Yes, Matthew has challenges. Yes, he does things differently. Yes, it may take him longer to accomplish a task, but no, that doesn't mean he can't achieve just about anything else you or I do on a daily basis.

To be honest, our family's whole life is very different. We have ramps on both the front and the back of our house (which were a godsend when we had a grandparent who used a walker or when we had an elderly dog who could no longer do the stairs). We have an accessible van, which sounds fun because we get to park close to things, but also requires extra space to allow for the lowering of the ramp, something other drivers don't appreciate. We travel with a three-foot and a six-foot portable ramp in our van to accommodate entry into some of the older facilities in our historic city of Richmond, Virginia that have been repurposed into restaurants or other places where social activities take place.

There is never anything spontaneous about us. We have to plan out EVERYTHING we do to make sure we have all the bases covered. For example, when we travel, I have a three-page checklist of items I need to remember to pack or to do prior to our departure to "guarantee" we'll have an easy, successful encounter at either the airport or our destination. I need to be certain Matthew will be comfortable on the airplane or, upon arrival, be able to accomplish his daily activities with ease. We never get to experience that moment of not "sweating the small stuff" because we always have to be looking outside of the box to accomplish simple things others take for granted.

We get frustrated sometimes because things aren't easy. Getting Matthew ready in the morning takes two hours. Trivial things like walking down the street can be a problem if curb cuts don't exist or if someone has parked in front of them creating a barrier to get from the sidewalk to the street. Sometimes a restaurant has created an outside café that blocks passage for someone in a wheelchair. Sometimes trash is piled where we need to go, or it has rained and a huge puddle has formed at the base of the curb cut. We have found that being on alert and constantly taking in life at 360 degrees can be quite exhausting.

Let me be very clear, though, I wouldn't change one aspect of my life. I have learned more about people and the world's genuineness from watching Matthew navigate life than I could have ever learned if I'd had two "normal" kids. I've had the privilege of witnessing life through a different lens. I see Matthew's experience as a lesson in humanity, as an educational tool. I don't see Matthew's disability as others see it. What they see is a stigma, the stigma of disability. What I see is a person who is just like everybody else, with a few minor variations.

I also find it fascinating when I experience that *there but for the grace of God, go I* moment. Those individuals, in their minds, see Matthew as something they will NEVER be. This could not be any further from the truth. As we move through life, all of us, at one time or another, experience disability. Look around you. How many people do you see wearing glasses? Do you consider these individuals to be disabled? Probably not, yet they all need an accommodation, just like a disabled individual, to get through life. Do you think any less of them because they can't see as well as you can? No, because glasses have become an accepted accommodation. So, if this is the case for glasses, then why would you think any less of someone just because they can't walk without assistance? It is the same basic concept, just tweaked a bit.

Everybody hopes for one thing: to live a long, active and productive life. Most of us will probably achieve this goal, but I doubt once you get older that you'll be as active or as productive as you'd like to be. It's called becoming elderly. More than likely, once you reach this stage in life, you will probably acquire some form of disability along the way. Maybe your legs aren't as strong as they once were and you need a walker or a wheelchair or a scooter to get around. Maybe it is your eyesight that is what gives you problems. Maybe it's your hearing that gives you difficulty. The bottom line is that as we get old, we become disabled. Among many other things, this is a fact of life.

Even if you are one of the lucky ones and don't experience the actual state of disability until you are advanced in age, you need to remember that everyone has their own 'little sack of rocks" that they carry with them. Everyone in life has troubles, be they physical or mental. Whether rich or poor, the heartaches of life escape no one. By keeping this in mind when we interact with others it helps to better understand that everyone has something to contribute. Take advantage of that; don't let the negative outshine the positive that a person may have to offer. In other words, DON'T JUDGE A BOOK BY THE COVER. Even a short story can tell an impactful tale.

Additionally, everyone needs to open their minds to the concept that **disability is the only minority you can join in the blink of an eye**. Any one of us, through accident, illness or age can become that person who people walk by in the store and give "the look". Denial of this notion will make it that much harder when the inevitable happens. We should all take steps now to help diminish the stigma of disability, so that when we reach that point in life, "the look" no longer exists.

My final thought is this: Matthew is an amazing individual. I have totally enjoyed spending the last 26 years watching him grow and navigate life. He deserves equal opportunity for any aspect of his life. He deserves the same level of respect that his co-worker gets. He deserves employment, friendships, relationships, opportunities, or attainable goals, just like anybody else. Simply because he uses a wheelchair to get from point A to point B, does not disqualify him from any options that life should offer.

Takeaways

1. Enjoy life to the fullest and appreciate every aspect of every day. Nothing should hold you back from achieving your ultimate goals in life. Look outside the box. Never say never.

2. Actions speak louder than words. That visible look in the store only exacerbates the stigma of disability. Think before you make expressions like that; the impact on individuals with disabilities can prevent them from getting a step ahead.

3. Remember (and follow) the Golden Rule: Do unto others as you would have them do unto you. Imagine how you'd feel if someone made that face as they walked by you? Self-image is a major aspect of everyone's life. Don't be the person who erodes another person's perception of themselves.

4. Don't judge a book by the cover. Never underestimate someone's abilities. Someone may not be able to walk, but his or her senses, as well as their aspirations, desires, and goals are just fine and deserve to be attained. Give them credit where credit is due. Allow them to grow and blossom. Give them a shot. Whatever doubt you may hold towards them, they'll destroy.

5. Be proactive, not reactive to difference. Be that person who goes out of their way to help, not the person who denies the existence of difference. Give everyone leeway and understanding so they can become the person they always knew the they could be.

7 Finding & Fulfilling: A Perspective on Your Path to Purpose

Derek Alan

The two most important days in your life are the day you are born and the day you find out why. -Mark Twain

Perhaps you might be in a season of life much like I was: questioning my purpose, searching for direction and trying to make sense of my past. Through an unfocused perspective, I felt as if I was drifting through life, uncertain, unsatisfied and unfulfilled. Asking myself questions like; Why didn't I get the job? Why did she walk away? What did I do to deserve this? What reason could all of this pain serve? The lack of answers and pressure from expectations to have it all figured out, were only reminders of my seemingly trivial pursuit.

In this chapter I am going to share a perspective that brought me peace on my path to purpose, one that will help you reflect on the past, provide encouragement for the present and inspire optimism for the future. Trust me, I know there are times where circumstances have made you resent what has happened or fear what might happen. However, when you realize we are all on a path to finding and fulfilling our purpose, the way you look at things changes. You no longer resent or fear your path but celebrate and welcome it. The following are a few things I have discovered along the way that have helped me do my part, make progress and avoid poisons on my path to purpose.

Before we begin, let me set the expectations straight for this chapter. Spoiler alert, I am not a purpose prophet. I do not have a crystal ball or the ability to see the future and tell you what your purpose is. Nor if I could, would I tell you. I like to consider myself more like a purpose Sherpa. If you are not familiar, a Sherpa is an experienced guide that helps climbers on their journey to the top of Mount Everest.

With that being said, I am going to make a disclaimer. Like the Sherpa, I am here to guide and help point you in the right direction, but you still have to do all the climbing. If you have not already come to this conclusion, allow me to be the one to break the news. There are no elevators to the top or piggyback rides to your destination. So just in case it was not clear the first time, you are responsible for all the climbing. That is so important that not only did I repeat it, but now I want you to repeat it. Out loud. Say it with me: "I am responsible for all the climbing". Ok, good, but I know you can do better. Let's do it again but this time loud enough so the people around you look at you a little funny. "I am responsible for all the climbing".

Now that we are on the same page (pun intended) and we have bonded over a small act of public humiliation, I feel we are good enough friends that I can ask you for a small favor. Before we dive into the rest of the chapter I would like you to reread the quote from Mark Twain at the start of the chapter. Then take a minute to let those words sink in because they hold a lot of truth.

It is hard to disagree about the first greatest day of your life, the day you were born. You may not remember much, but you changed the world just by entering it. If you have a hard time believing this, just ask your parents, siblings or best friend. I can guarantee you their worlds changed. However, the second greatest day of your life is much more elusive and takes a little longer than nine months. As human as it is to be born, so is the desire to find out why. The question that has been at the center of the human condition for thousands of years: Why am I here? What is my purpose? Once again, I cannot give you the answer to this question but I can offer some advice to guide you along the way.

Doing your P.A.R.T.

On the path to finding and fulfilling your purpose, you have to do your part. As you can see, I didn't say you have to do it alone. You will encounter people and resources along the way that will help you on your journey. However, living your purpose does not come about by happenstance or accident. You must be intentional. Every day is filled with thousands of choices but are you being intentional with your decisions?

Maybe you have been lured into believing the same illusion I fell victim to for so many years. Despite common belief, in life we have control over very little. The majority of what lies out of our control is a product of the people and circumstances of our environment. Some take this fact and use it as an excuse. In reality, this fact reveals an even stronger truth.

Yes, we may not get to choose what happens to us but we do get to choose how we respond to it. The following is a guide to making sure you are doing your P.A.R.T. on your path to purpose.

Pick

As mentioned, we do not have control over many of the things in our lives. However, what we do have control over makes all the difference. Three of the most important things each and every one of us has control over is our actions, reactions and thoughts. In order to do your part, you must first realize that you and only you get to pick your actions, reactions and thoughts. Never forget—you get to pick.

Actions

As you verbally proclaimed moments ago, you are responsible for all the climbing. This also includes all the walking, heavy lifting and don't forget to do a little dancing. What I am really trying to say is, it is up to you to take action. Like every journey, your path to purpose is made up of steps or actions that need to be taken to reach your destination. The good news is, you're in control of your actions; you make the decisions. This also means you can choose not to act. Action or inaction—you get to pick.

Reactions

Reactions, as the word suggests, are very similar to actions. If I was going to relate the two I would call them siblings. The main difference between them is that reactions are direct responses to another action. This introduces a wild card into the equation that is often out of our control. For example, certain actions like being cut off in traffic, your flight being cancelled or getting dumped, are all things we do not choose to happen to us. But guess what? We do get to pick how we react to them.

Thoughts

So, if actions and reactions are siblings, thoughts would be their mother. Your thoughts give birth to all of your actions and reactions. This makes your thoughts the most important part of doing your P.A.R.T. on your path to purpose. How you perceive and interpret the world around you creates your reality. Ironically, this is the area we put the least amount of thought toward. How often do you think about the way you think? Unlike actions and reactions, you do not get to pick every one of your thoughts. Emotions, fears and other people are really good at making suggestions on how you should think. However, you do get to pick whether or not you believe them.

In summary, we do not have control over the landscape on our path to purpose but we do have a lot of choices that will influence it. Pick wisely. Now that you understand how to do your P.A.R.T., you are ready to make progress on your path. The next section will present three steps proven to help you make progress to finding and fulfilling your purpose.

Making Progress

Whether you are still in search of or have already realized your purpose, there are many times it seems you are not making any progress on your path. The days pass one after another with little show. All of a sudden, you have stalled or strayed from your path. The days turn into weeks, weeks accumulate into months and years later, you find yourself asking, "How did I get here?" You may wake up one day and ask this question but it does not happen overnight. It happens a little each day you're not intentional about picking your actions, reactions and thoughts. There are many reasons that cause us to drift from our paths and prevent us from fulfilling our purpose but I will discuss those further in the next section.

Just like any other journey, your path to purpose is going to be taken one step at a time. The equation to making progress is simple— place one foot in front of the other and repeat. You are probably saying to yourself, "thanks for the advice but I already know how to walk". Great! Now for the hard part, actually taking the steps. Again, how to make progress is simple but I never said it was going to be easy. We have all been there. You know exactly what you need to do and you know exactly how to do it but we fail to take the actions or steps necessary to accomplish what lies before us.

Through trial and error (believe me, there have been plenty of errors) I have learned that there are three P's to progress.

Prepare   *Prior preparation prevents poor performance.*
             James Baker
Participate *You miss 100% of the shots you don't take. Wayne Gretzky*

Persevere *Success is not final, failure is not fatal: it is the courage to continue that counts. Winston Churchill*

Now do not think your progress will be complete by taking these steps only once? That would be similar to believing you can finish a marathon after the first three steps. You must prepare, participate and persevere perpetually on your path to purpose. Over and over again, day in and day out. Do this enough times and I promise you will run into the fourth P of Progress. You will eventually get pretty damn lucky, because as the old saying goes, *luck is the point where preparation meets opportunity*.

As mentioned above, there are many reasons that can prevent you from making progress on your path. Most of the time, distractions or busyness is the culprit. However, another reason you're failing to make progress on your path is that you could be poisoned. Not literally, but the life and death of your purpose is in the balance.

Poison Control

Unfortunately, we are living in a world where many have confused these poisons with their purpose. They have placed these fleeting and self-serving desires above what they have been created and called to do. This is by no means an exhaustive list but a few of the most common:

Pride

Let me clarify. There is nothing wrong with taking pride in one's work, appearance or accomplishments. Actually, it would be more concerning if you were not proud of yourself or your achievements. That being said, there is a difference between a sense of satisfaction and a sense of arrogance. Pride is not the issue, it is excessive pride. You see, pride does not become poisonous until you are so full of it, you have no room left for humility. I think that is why they call it being prideful.

Partying

We all know the type of behavior I am talking about. It is the unmoderated, overindulgentparticipation in actions that we know are unhealthy and harmful. This reckless lifestyle is not only unhealthy for one's physical well-being but also for relationships, finances and careers. Obviously, drugs and alcohol come to mind but any fashion of wild living can be a poison on your path to purpose. The temptations sound sweet but the pleasure is temporary and the taste of the consequences are bitter.

Possessions

Let me see if you can relate to this situation. Have you ever wanted a new (insert item here)? Do you remember how excited and happy you were when you finally got the item? Do you also remember how you felt weeks or months later when the next version came out, a new fashion line was released or one of your friends got something else you liked even better? Chances are, you were feeling a lot less grateful and now desiring the newest or next thing. This is the trap you fall into when you make your life about possessions and not your purpose. I believe wholeheartedly that the impact of your purpose will be greater than anything else you leave behind in this world.

Again, these are only a few of the poisons we all encounter on our path. For some, it can be seeking popularity. For others, it can be the pursuit of pleasure or a paycheck. Please do not misunderstand me. By no means am I saying not to attend New Year's parties or that it's a crime to make a good living or it's wrong to own nice things. However, when your desire for these things is greater than the desire for your purpose, that is when they become poisonous.

Consider this your warning because these poisons will prevent you from pursuing your purpose. By allowing these poisons to take priority over your purpose, you are doing an injustice to yourself and a disservice to the world. The next section will present a few principles to guide you along your path to avoid these poisons and pursue your purpose.

Pathway Principles to Practice

As you are following your path toward finding and fulfilling your purpose, I have found the following eight principles to be universal and essential:

Personal Promise

This is a promise to yourself to be your best self, the person you continually need to become in order to fulfill your purpose. On my path, there were many times I was guilty of trying to be someone I was not. Then I decided to take Oscar Wilde's advice, "Be yourself; everyone else is already taken".

Pursue your Passion

Passion is the compass on your path to purpose. It is no coincidence that you are excited about certain topics or you have interests in a specific activity. Things of great significance are rarely achieved without passion and there is no greater significance than fulfilling your purpose. Follow your passion and you will find your purpose.

Positive Perspective

Do you see problems or possibilities? Is your path a prison or a paradise? Are you living in poverty or in prosperity? There is power in a positive perspective; it may not change your circumstances but it will change how you respond to them. As an ancient proverb says, "Be careful how you think, your life is shaped by your thoughts".

Pledge of Patience

If there is one thing you want to pack plenty of on your path to purpose, it is patience—particularly, patience for the process and patience for people. Finding and fulling your purpose takes a lifetime, so you need to be patient and trust the process. Along the way, you will also meet people who are as imperfect as you are. Patience will be required.

Priority Planning

As Benjamin Franklin once said, "If you fail to plan, you are planning to fail". It is essential on your path to purpose to set goals and write out steps to achieve them. With no priorities, how will you know what is most important? Setting goals makes your vision actionable, your progress trackable and provides clarity for decision-making.

Pay the Price

Please forgive me. I forgot to mention that your path to purpose is a toll road and it is not cheap. The price is not paid with spare change, dollars or a sticker on your windshield. It's paid with the sacrifice of time, comfort, certainty, sleep, relationships, resources and most of all, who you used to be. Who you were and currently are must give way to who you are becoming

Persistent Prayer

Regardless of being a person of faith, having an attitude of gratitude is needed on your path. It is being thankful for what you have, where you are and what you can do. This mindset is much more productive to finding and fulfilling your purpose than the alternative.

Paramount Picture

Any purpose that is not greater than yourself is a tragic misuse of your time, talents and gifts. If you do not believe me, let's do the math. If you are the sole reason for your purpose, how many people are you impacting? One. However, when your purpose is outside yourself, your impact becomes immeasurably greater. On your path to purpose, you will realize—it's not about me, it's about meaning.

The Proposition

The intention of this chapter was not to persuade but merely to provide a personal philosophy. A perspective that helped me realize this: your path to purpose starts on a journey to finding yourself and ends on a mission fulfilling a purpose greater than yourself. To get the most out of what you read I would like to make a proposition. I highly encourage you to find a partner and also have them read the chapter. Then, over the next five weeks, meet to discuss one of the takeaways below. I firmly believe that this will magnify what you have learned and have a truly powerful effect as you continue down your path to purpose.

Takeaways

1. It is hard to disagree about the first greatest day of your life, the day you were born. You may not remember much, but you changed the world just by entering it. Understanding now that your past is preparation for your purpose, how has this changed your perspective on some of the events and experiences you had along your path?

2. On the path to finding and fulfilling your purpose, you have to do your part. Have you been doing your P.A.R.T.? What area do you think needs the most improvement when it comes to being more intentional about picking your actions, reactions and thoughts?

3. Just like any other journey, your path to purpose is going to be taken one step at a time. How can you implement the three steps discussed in the chapter to make progress on your path to purpose?

4. Poisons will prevent you from pursuing your purpose. By allowing these poisons to take priority over your purpose, you are doing an injustice to yourself and a disservice to the world. What are some of the poisons in your life that are preventing you from pursuing your purpose?

5. As you are following your path toward finding and fulfilling your purpose, some principles are universal and essential. Which Pathway Principle most resonated with you and how will it help you in finding and fulfilling your purpose?

8 From Tailspin to Olympian: The Made-For-TV Movie that was my Real Life!

Sherry Winn

How many times have you believed that you were spinning out of control in an emotional tailspin? Have you fallen so far that climbing out of your hole feels next to impossible? Have you ever felt hopelessness? Experienced betrayal? Suffered abandonment? I've felt all those emotions and, on more than one occasion, wondered if life was worth the effort. If I had succumbed to those negative emotions, I would have never been an All-American Olympian or a National Championship basketball coach.

My tailspin begins in high school. I am an all-state athlete in three sports—softball, basketball, and volleyball. I am a straight A student, the golden child, and super girl on the basketball court. I am everything a parent desires—expecting love, adoration, and acknowledgment from my parents in return.

What can go wrong? I have everything, or so it seems from the outside looking in, but you never really know anybody else's story. You just think you do.

My story begins with my mom. Before I tell you about my family, please understand that when people are experiencing a crisis, they sometimes hurt other people, even people they love. And know that you might also hurt those you love when in despair. ***The greatest gift you can give to your loved ones and yourself is moving beyond the past.***

Picture yourself as the daughter of the coach. You are about to get into a van headed to the state softball tournament. You yell, "shotgun" at the same time another player does. As you climb into the van, your mom says, "What the heck do you think you're doing? Pam called shotgun. Get in the back seat." Pam is our shortstop—a great one. She can bumble the ball three times and still throw the runner out at first base, using her rocket arm. My mom adores her and the team loves her rocket arm. Pam also curses, drinks, smokes, and she barely passed her classes in high school.

I shrug my shoulders and get in the back seat stuffed between three other players, cleats, gloves, and bats. Pam, in the coveted shotgun position, is in control of the radio. In 1979, the only form of entertainment we had was the radio and on a long trip, the radio was everything. Pam plays 30 seconds of a song, switches the channel, and does this repeatedly—driving the rest of us crazy.

I say, "Hey Pam, could you please let us listen to an entire song, just once? P..L..E..A..S..E!" My mother jumps out of the van, runs around the van, throws open the door, and yells, "Out!" I climb out, leaving the van door wide-open. "What DO you THINK you are doing? You hurt Pam's feelings! APOLOGIZE!"

I roll my eyes and say, "Shit mom! By asking her to play a song to the end?" She yells, "Don't you ever curse at me, young lady! We don't curse in this family!"

Pam and my mother seem to have a connection that my mother and I do not have. To my mother, Pam is the golden child. Two weeks later, I sit at the dining room table doing homework, and Pam is visiting AGAIN. I can see, through the doorway, my mother and Pam in the living room, giggling and laughing, huddled together, sharing some inside joke. Then my mother does something that is forbidden in our house and in our family—she shoots Pam the finger! And Pam laughs. I feel betrayed, abandoned, lonely, and not good enough to be my mom's daughter and I hate myself, because I am not good enough, in any way, for my mom to love me.

Maybe you have felt that you were not good enough for your father or mother—somewhere in your life, you've felt betrayed or abandoned. Maybe your brother or sister was the golden child and you were the afterthought. ***If you've ever felt that way, know you are not alone, and the person who betrayed you is in crisis.***

Three months later, I am in college on a full basketball scholarship at the University of Houston, and completely incapable of playing basketball or going to classes, because I am too busy hating myself. I am catapulted into a new world. I come from a lily-white neighborhood where the minority are the ones with only three-bedroom homes. In college, I am the minority on the basketball team, and I am naïve.

I say to my roommate: "My grandfather used to roll his cigarettes that way too, but his tobacco was always brown."

I ask my suitemate, "Do we have a water crisis?"

"No, Why?"

"Because my roommate and her boyfriend conserved water today. They took a shower together."

I ask my teammates if their hair is black because they iron it all the time. I don't say this because I am racist. I say it because I am ignorant. I am naïve and I say stupid things. I'm learning fast what it is like to be in a minority. When I hang out with the other white player on the team, Kay, my black teammates stop talking to me. I ask Muffy, "What is going on? Why aren't y'all talking to me anymore?"

"You don't want to hang around Kay. She is gay."

I reply, "I like people who laugh and have fun."

I AM still naïve. What I don't understand though is, if you are considered a minority, why would you disown, point out, or judge another minority group? **Why would you give the same experience that you hate?**

Then, in the middle of the semester, I understood. At a bar, I see one of my former high school softball opponents. I say, "Hey Janice." Janice says, "I can't believe you are at this bar." "Yeah...I know. I am not the nice kid anymore. I DRINK." She says, "No, I thought you were like your mom. You know, I thought you would be at the gay bar."

Like a tsunami, the realization hits me—my 40-year-old mom and my 17-year-old teammate are lovers. And I HATE them. I feel betrayed, unloved, confused, unsupported, and most of all, I fear I am just like my mom. That night, I drink and drink and drink. Drink and the pain will go away. *Drink and you can forget. Drink and you will wake up a different person.* The situation with my mom *led* me to drink.

Have you ever been "driven to drink" because of a conflict with your partner, friend, parents, or siblings? To avoid facing an issue? Out of anger, frustration, failure or because you wanted to be funny, liked, or admired? Have you ever had too much to drink to escape, even if just for a few hours?

During the basketball season, I rarely got to play and I blamed it on my coach. I transferred to Texas A&M and ran away from my heartaches. Do you know why running away is a problem? The problem is that, wherever you go, you always take yourself with you. And when you don't like yourself, other people don't like you either. They find ways to exclude you, subtly and not so subtly, which is exactly what happened to me.

After riding the bench at the University of Houston, I move home and get my act together. I lose the extra six-pack I gained from self-medicating with alcohol. I work out every day—running, weight-training, and shooting. I am ready to KICK ASS and nobody is going to stop me!

On the Aggie basketball team, I am a starter and the top scorer, averaging 17 points per game, yet I am still unlovable. Imagine sitting on a bus with your teammates and nobody will sit next to you. Imagine going to eat and your teammates race to the table so they don't have to sit next to you. Imagine playing basketball and your teammates pass the ball to your opponents before they will pass it to you!

After the first ten games, with me leading the team in scoring and assists, my teammates tell my coach, "We can't play with Sherry. She is too selfish. She only cares about herself." My coach sits in her office, leans back in her black leather chair, looks at me, and says, "You are the best player I've ever coached. You could be All-American, but if you can't get along with your teammates, you can't play here."

"I'm willing to get along. I'll do anything to get along."

Coach gets up from behind her desk and says, "Let's go talk to the team." She puts me in front of the team, without any conflict resolution rules, and says, "Tell Sherry how you feel about her." This instruction is like throwing ten pounds of dead fish in a shark tank and then asking you to jump in, or like hanging a deer carcass around your neck and throwing you into the lion's den.

Kelly says, "You are not a team player and you will never be a team player." Tammy says, "You think you are better than all of us, but you are not. You just think you are." I look at my coach, begging her silently to say something, to intervene, to provide some sort of road map for conversing. She stands silent. And finally, the words that break me, "Even if you change, I still won't like you. You are just the kind of person who isn't likeable." People tend to shrug off words but, *I am here to tell you that words cut, they make you bleed, they wound you so deeply that the scars last a lifetime.*

I walk out, quit the team, and start drinking. I drink for two weeks straight. This is where my tailspin spirals out of control to a nearly fatal level. I wake up, drink until I pass out, and then start the process again. In the middle of my two-week drunk, I wake up in the middle of the night to go the bathroom and discover my partner having sex with my friend. I don't say a word, turn, walk out of the room, and grab another drink. I am already the *walking dead*. Nothing else can hurt me.

The next day, I meet a man at a bar (I still don't know what his name is to this day.) Mister *whatchamacallit* says, "Hey baby, did you sit in a pile of sugar? Cause you sure have a pretty sweet ass!" I look at him and say, "You might be an ass for saying that, but I let asses buy me drinks. Whiskey. Straight up."

After three shots of whiskey, Mr. *whatchamacallit* says, "You want to go on a breakfast date?"

"Nope."

"We'll have Budweiser for breakfast."

"Tell me more."

"And we are going to shoot clay pigeons."

Booze and guns. What Texas girl wouldn't say yes to that as a first date? The next morning, we drink our breakfast as we drive to *whatchamacallit's* friend's house. The house is more like a shed, a shack, or Cujo's doghouse. I meet *whatchamacallit's* friends, Dick and Jane, and Grandpa. Okay, so I don't remember their names either.

We shoot at the clay pigeons for a while without much success, but the idea of shooting something makes me feel good. When lunch rolls around, we drink more beer and smoke a couple of joints. Afterwards, we sit on the back porch and shoot whatever is in sight—buckets, rakes, shovels, wheel barrows, the lawn mower, the chickens…everything except the dogs. Even in that crazed state of mind, I can't shoot a dog. I love dogs. I could never hurt a dog, and I still feel bad about the chickens.

I don't remember much about that day, but I do remember Dick and Jane's kid in diapers, and us sitting at the kitchen table inhaling through a bong, their baby hungry and crying, and us smoking pot and laughing. Even though I am out of it, I know not taking care of the kid is wrong.

I decide to go for a walk to clear my mind and Grandpa decides to go with me, uninvited. Grandpa smiles through his front tooth and says, "Hey honeybunch, cutie-pie, strawberry pickle."

"Strawberry pickle?"

He points at his body and says, "What would it take to get you to want some of this?"

I look at Grandpa's front tooth and the five days of stubble on his chin, and say, "A mansion, a Maserati, a million dollars."

Grandpa pinches me on the butt. I swat his hand away and say, "You don't own a Maserati, do you?" He reaches for my boob. I swat his hand away and say, "NOT FOR SALE." Grandpa leans in like he's going to kiss me, and I say, "No way, José! Not now. Not ever."

Do you understand that "no means no" and does not stand for never-ending opportunity? When somebody says "no" to you, don't try to make it a "yes"—not with your words, not with your hands, not with your lips, not with your body.

Grandpa grabs my shoulders and tries to pull me into him, I use my well-honed muscles to push him. He falls off the step backwards and slams his head on the concrete. My CPR training kicks in. "Grandpa. Grandpa. Grandpa. Are you okay?" When he doesn't respond, I run into the house.

"Hey y'all, your dad hit his head. He is out cold on the concrete. He fell and hit his head." They shrug and keep inhaling. "Yeah, he will be all right. His head is the toughest thing on him."

"He is bleeding. Unconscious."

"Good. We will have peace and quiet for a while."

Finally, I convince them to go outside. They pick Grandpa up and throw him on a couch without thoughts of a hospital, a doctor, or an ER, then they go back to the bong and beer. You might want to know what happened to Grandpa and the kid. I wish I could tell you. I don't know. I blacked out. Some people might tell you that not knowing is good, but I am here to tell you that every day, I wish I knew what happened to Grandpa and the kid.

The next morning, when I wake up, I don't go for a drink. I go for my .38 snub-nosed special. I pick up the pistol and place the barrel under my chin. I sit with my finger on the trigger for an hour. Do you know what stops me from pulling the trigger? I'm afraid that, with my luck, I won't kill myself. I'll survive with greater injuries.

I take the bullets out of the pistol, lock it back up, and decide that if I remain in this emotional state, I am not going to exist for long. I need to change and I need to change NOW.

I am living proof that you don't have to stay who you are, you can get better. You can do something different, be somebody different, improve, and love who you are. Three years from that date, I am marching into the Opening Ceremonies of the 1984 Olympic Games. How did I get to the Olympics? I pivoted and turned.

When is it time for you to pivot and turn? And how do you get there? I didn't change in an hour, a day, or a week. If you want instant gratification to change the essence of you, you will be disappointed. If you can just move six inches today toward where you want to go, you will arrive at your destination. You can do the same things I did daily: *read something positive, repeat affirmations, visualize your future, express gratitude daily, and forgive yourself and others.*

I probably never would have made the Olympic basketball team, but when that door was so firmly shut in front of me, I PIVOTED to a new direction—a direction that led me to two Olympic Games. Sometimes the door that is shut in front of you is exactly what you need to get you where you need to be to reach your goals.

Takeaways

1. Understand that judging yourself through other people's words renders you powerless.

2. Acknowledge that interpreting other people's motives and words is impossible.

3. Realize that self-medicating with alcohol doesn't resolve your issues.

4. Comprehend that you can't run away from your problems, because you might be part of the issue.

5. Recognize that you can pivot and turn at any time in your life to a better you.

9 Live Beyond Limits
Erin McCamley

As we let our own light shine, we unconsciously give other people permission to do the same. As we're liberated from our own fear, our presence automatically liberates others. -Marianne Williamson

      I had an experience in college that was, unfortunately, not unique at all, but fundamentally altered my life. Like one in three women on this planet, I am a survivor of sexual violence. I was raped by a fellow freshman my freshman year, and reported it that night. I had to tell my story, while I was in shock, to several people that night, most of them in uniform. I then had to tell my story countless more times, several times a day, every few days, for the next nine months, which was exhausting. The event itself was traumatizing, obviously; he violated my body, which I carry around with me 24/7, so I have to relive my worst event all the time. However, what also changed my life forever was the nine-month long investigation that followed, during which I was interrogated, bullied, and blamed at every turn.

      I suffer from Post-Traumatic Stress Disorder, or PTSD, because of it. This experience altered my worldview in many ways, but it wasn't just the event itself—it was also the aftermath and people's reaction to the event that turned my world upside down. Survivors of sexual violence often get PTSD, but very few ever know that, because of how dismissed and blamed they often are. There is a stigma surrounding mental illness in general, and PTSD from sexual violence is no exception. In the best-case scenario, many people believe a victim should be able to "get over" what happened to them at some point—and in the worst-case scenario, many people believe the victim deserved it in some way.

      Whether a survivor of sexual violence develops PTSD or not, they suffer lifelong issues: depression, anxiety, trust issues, self-sabotage, alcohol and drug abuse, self-harm, suicidal thoughts, anger issues that can manifest in explosive outbursts caused by seemingly small things, breakdowns when reminded of the event in any way, and more. The investigation ended with my rapist receiving a slap on the wrist; and even though all I asked was that he be kicked off campus so I could feel safe, they wouldn't do that because it "happened behind closed doors" (where else does almost every rape happen, by the way?) and thus they couldn't prove it—so I had to see my attacker every few days for the next four years.

Why was the aftermath of this terrible event so negative, and the outcome so unsatisfying? In the judicial system and disciplinary systems in schools, why is so much time and effort spent on how the victim contributed to what happened—what was she wearing, was she drinking? Why is this the one crime where, when it is reported, the starting assumption is that the accuser is lying? According to the U.S. Department of Justice, "Law enforcement agencies indicate that about 8% of forcible rapes reported to them were determined to be unfounded."

This is in line with false reporting for crimes overall, and yet the credibility of the victim of sexual assault is challenged and questioned throughout the process. The likelihood that the victim will be blamed and attacked during the investigation undoubtedly contributes to the fact that only 32% of sexual assaults are even reported in the first place. I understand the concept of "innocent until proven guilty", but when someone reports a robbery, the police don't automatically start barraging them with questions about how they contributed to being robbed, ultimately deciding it's their fault. The investigation opened my eyes to a lot of deep-seated, unquestioned values about gender that are built into our thinking. Are these deep-seated, deeply conditioned beliefs about gender why sexual violence is so common? One in three women will experience sexual violence during their lifetime, which is 1.2 billion women worldwide.

I decided early on that, even though I had no control over what happened to me, I could control my response. I decided that I would talk about what happened and the impact on me. There was no reason for me to be ashamed or embarrassed. If anyone should be ashamed, it is the guy who raped me, and the people who treated me so poorly afterward. One way to reduce stigma is to show people how ridiculous it is to stigmatize a victim.

I also decided that I would learn as much as I could about this issue, to educate myself and others. In doing my own investigation, I learned that the issue with the system that deals with sexual violence is much more than just a problem of "He said, she said." It is an issue with beliefs and attitudes about gender and sex. These beliefs and attitudes damage us beyond just sexual violence and its victims. They place limits on us when it comes to choosing a career, whether or not we choose healthy relationships, whether we believe we deserve self-care or not, and more. This realization got me thinking.

Where do limits come from? Who puts limits on us?

There are so many external forces, it's hard to identify them, but conditioning begins at birth. We're given different tools based on our gender, race, class, and ability. The first limits begin with toys, words, and colors. If our parents can afford toys, we're given toys based on our gender that indirectly teach us things about what we should like and be drawn to. Then we're directly told things about how we should be with words: "Little boys don't do that." "Little girls don't do that." "Don't get your pretty dress dirty playing in the mud, honey." Girls' rooms are painted pink or purple, boys' rooms are painted blue or green, and they get matching toys; so, as we grow, we know to reach and ask for toys of those colors. If you want to test this, point to a blue toy and ask any 5-year-old girl if that's for her or her brother (or some male cousin) and listen to her response. These toys teach us things about how we should be. Girls' toys are about the home and being pretty (dolls, kitchen sets, makeup) and boys' toys are about achievement and brain development (superheroes, racecars, Legos).

Then we go to school where our peers and teachers enforce these limits and introduce new ones. It becomes even scarier to be different. But we're also told platitudes all the time that send a conflicting message, like "always be yourself" and "you are the only you on Earth, so be you." Once we're adults, we have a fairly strong sense of self, and we are told we can make choices and be who we want to be. So, who puts limits on us now?

Don't we have free will? Don't we make choices?

The answer is, of course, we do—but it can be extremely difficult to recognize limits that come from outside us. It is so hard to stand back, look at all the information that has been driven into us literally since birth, question it, and choose our own answers. For a grown man, it is more than a little difficult to reprogram yourself to believe that having emotions and openly weeping is okay. (In fact, it is more than okay—it requires more strength to confront an emotion than to suppress and run from it, actually, but that is a conversation for another day.) For a grown woman, it is more than a little difficult to reprogram yourself to believe that you can be the protagonist of your own story, since you have never seen that before. You can put yourself first; in fact, you <u>must</u> in order be helpful to others. You know that "put your own oxygen mask on before assisting others" announcement on airplanes? There's a good reason for that safety instruction. But women are taught their whole lives to put others first, which means to never think of yourself, because that would mean you're selfish. But how can you be helpful to others if you have no energy left?

If we don't question what we've been taught, we will be boxed in by limits we don't even know are there. We will regurgitate what previous generations taught us and, even when we have a sneaking suspicion that we don't agree with something, we will plow forward. We will give up on dreams we don't even know we have before we begin.

How can we become aware of limits placed on us, and start to live a life beyond those limits? I recommend following these 5 steps to Live Beyond Limits!

Step 1 - *Question* what you know and accept as facts about yourself and your life.

Question what you know! To begin to live beyond limits, you have to believe it is possible to do so—dream big! Believe that you have access to many more opportunities than you currently think are possible. We have to break down visible and invisible barriers and limits. Do you want to be a brain surgeon? Did you just laugh when you read that sentence? Why did you laugh? Because you're not smart enough? Because you're too busy? Because you don't have the money to pursue the education necessary to become a brain surgeon? Because no one in your family got an education, so why would you? Instead of just accepting these things as facts, question them. Break them apart. There are many brain surgeons out there, some of whom may have started out less qualified than you. They pursued their dream, why not you?

Step 2 - *Realize* that many limits are self-imposed and based in fear.

You are the source of many of the limits in your life. Certainly, some barriers and limits are imposed on us by external forces: society, our culture, where we live. Often it is easier to blame outside forces, because then we are not personally responsible. But deep down it's usually fear that holds us back. Fear of our own greatness. There is a famous quote by author Marianne Williamson from her book A Return to Love that states, "Our deepest fear is not that we are inadequate. Our deepest fear is that we are powerful beyond measure. It is our light, not our darkness that most frightens us. We ask ourselves, who am I to be brilliant, gorgeous, talented, and fabulous? Actually, who are you not to be?"

It is our responsibility to bring our special gifts and abilities to the world and not hide them away in a 9-5 job that we hate because we feel we don't deserve better, or we are too afraid to do better. If that 9-5 job is exactly what you want, then go for it, of course. But if you are following the script: "go to school, get a job, make enough money to live in my house and afford my car to drive to work, and be too tired to do anything fun, and hopefully live long enough to retire and then start living, but probably I'll die of stress before then and have wasted my life, but oh well I did the American dream", then I suggest you start questioning the structure of your life. It's never too late to change the course if you want—or, more accurately, need—to start actually living.

Step 3 - *Identify* beliefs from internal and external sources that hold you back.

Think about deep-seated beliefs that guide your actions and how you think about yourself. Are these your beliefs that you have come to after careful thought and reflection? Or are they beliefs you were told and taught at home and school that you accept as your own? To break through limits, you need to break down beliefs that hold you back, especially as they pop up throughout the process of going after what you want. This is not a one and done thing. We have to combat these conditioned beliefs from inner and outer forces almost daily. If you're one of the 1 in 4 males who are a victim of domestic violence in your lifetime, your pain or PTSD may be erased—or worse, laughed at—because men are supposed to be "the stronger ones" who are incapable of being abused. If you're a straight male in high school who dreams of being a ballet dancer, you're likely to be met with quite a bit of resistance—because being a ballet dancer is for girls, right? And apparently, the worst thing you can be in this world is a girl. Think of all those insults people hurl around when they perceive someone as weak, nagging, cowardly, or overly emotional ("pussy", "b*tch"). They're all gender specific. You have to recognize and resist the beliefs that are built into our very *language*.

Hey, I didn't say this was going to be easy!

Step 4 - *Determine* what you want for yourself and your life.

In order to live beyond limits, you will need to figure out what you actually want. What kind of person do you want to be? What kind of life do you want to live? In order to begin answering these questions, I recommend using motivational coach Jen Sincero's method from her book You are a Badass. Ask yourself this question:

If I had all the money and resources in the world, what would I spend my time doing?

And then spend your time doing that. That dream is what you were put on earth to do, and you will struggle financially, spiritually, and otherwise until you are in alignment with your purpose. "But I need to feel financially secure first before I go chasing childish dreams," you say. I hear you; that's been beaten into us since birth too. But strangely, it seems to work in the reverse. Only when you risk it and leap for the dream, the thing you were put here to do, will doors actually open for you, financial and otherwise.

Step 5 - *Take* concrete actions to pursue your dream and purpose.

And the fifth step to overcoming limits is to start taking concrete actions to go for it – to go after what you want for yourself and your life. This leads to the scariest thought of all: What if you take the leap and fail? What if the big dream doesn't work out? Is it better to live a "life of death," as Sufi poet Rumi would put it, than to "die on the rocks" after taking the leap? Is it better to be comfortable but not happy than to be happy but possibly uncomfortable? These are questions you have to ask yourself over and over again as you pursue your dreams. You deserve a life of joy, not of bland comfort. If you've been taught otherwise, now is your chance to learn something new.

At a certain point in our lives, as functioning, conscious, rational, thinking humans, it becomes our responsibility to question things and build our own lives. At some point, we either continue putting limits on ourselves or we break free. We can no longer blame others.

My PTSD affects my daily life—I get triggered easily even a decade after being raped. I struggle with depression and a tendency to self-sabotage. But when I came to recognize these damaging, far-reaching beliefs about gender that caused so much pain, oppression, limitation, and suppression in the world, I decided it was my responsibility to do something about them. Even though it is extremely painful to write about my story and my experience, I do it because I feel it will bring enlightenment to fellow survivors and to attackers. Even though it is extremely painful to talk about beliefs that perpetuate what is known as "rape culture," the culture that empowers and protects rapists and belittles and shames victims, I do it because I feel it is necessary to educate others before change can happen. I refuse to be limited by my attacker, by my experiences, or by society. The more open I am about my experience, the more I can heal and bring healing to others. Although healing may not be comfortable, it is full of light, adventure, and joy, and therefore I welcome it. I choose to Live Beyond Limits!

While going through these 5 steps to Live Beyond Limits, ask yourself these questions: If you see something lacking in your life, do you have the courage to change it? Do you have the courage to question your deeply held beliefs to break free? Do you have the courage to live the life you profoundly deserve?

Takeaways

1. Know the 5 steps to follow to Live Beyond Limits!

2. Become aware of limits placed on us.

3. Learn where limits come from.

4. Learn statistics about sexual violence and its far-reaching impact.

5. Be able to identify several types of conditioning revolving around gender in your daily life and in the media.

CHAPTER NOTES

1.) One in three women will experience sexual and/or domestic violence in their lifetime.

    a. "It is estimated that 35 per cent of women worldwide have experienced either physical and/or sexual intimate partner violence or sexual violence by a non-partner at some point in their lives. However, some national studies show that up to 70 per cent of women have experienced physical and/or sexual violence from an intimate partner in their lifetime" [1] World Health Organization, Department of Reproductive Health and Research, London School of Hygiene and Tropical Medicine, South African Medical Research Council (2013). Global and regional estimates of violence against women: prevalence and health effects of intimate partner violence and non-partner sexual violence, p.2.

2.) Survivors of sexual violence often get PTSD, but very few ever know that because of how dismissed and blamed they often are.

    a. Web page: (https://www.ptsd.va.gov/public/ptsd-overview/women/sexual-assault-females.asp) has great information on immediate and long-term effects of sexual violence, and here is the specific portion on rape victims' tendency to get PTSD (a study concluded 1 in 3 rape victims develop PTSD at some point in their lifetime):

    b. PTSD: Post-traumatic Stress Disorder (PTSD) involves a pattern of symptoms that some individuals develop after experiencing a traumatic event such as sexual assault. Symptoms of PTSD include repeated thoughts of the assault; memories and nightmares; avoidance of thoughts, feelings, and situations related to the assault; negative changes in thought and feelings; and increased arousal (for example difficulty sleeping and concentrating, jumpiness, irritability). One study that examined PTSD symptoms among women who were raped found that almost all (94 out of 100) women experienced these symptoms during the two weeks immediately following the rape. Nine months later, about 30 out of 100 of the women were still reporting this pattern of symptoms. The National Women's Study reported that almost one of every three all rape victims develop PTSD sometime during their lives.

3.) Conditioning/gender-typing
    a.   This article references a lot of different studies and materials: https://jezebel.com/5561837/girls-are-pink-boys-are-blue-on-toddlers-and-gender-roles

4.) Gender biases
    a.   This National Bureau of Economic Research paper discusses gender biases in readings, teacher's examples, everyday dialogue, etc. and the long-term effects of gender conditioning in young and developing minds: http://www.nber.org/papers/w20909

5.) Statistic: 1 in 4 men are victims of domestic violence
    a.   Source: National Coalition Against Domestic Violence (and others) and can be found here: https://ncadv.org/statistics

10 Coming to America
Luda Pirrmann

Whatever happens in our lives has its own reason or purpose. We experience suffering and happiness, failing and winning, falling and rising, sadness and celebration. All of these are the many faces of life. No matter what, this changing game never stops. Life goes on—welcome and embrace. Enjoy the ride.

Coming to America is the best thing that ever happened to me. Through divorce, I have cried a river of tears with hope and desperation. I have prayed to invisible forces to save my family from breaking apart. But now, looking back, a thought comes to mind that I was blessed without being consciously aware of the blessing. Life has invited me to write a new chapter. I accepted the challenge, and a serendipitous unfolding of the future began.

My parents kept saying, "You are still young and should find someone to love and have a family again." At the age of 34, and after my first marriage fell apart, I did not want to even think of getting married again. Since my divorce, a nagging depression still had its grip on me, but Mom and Dad wanted so much to see me being happy again, so I agreed to do something about it.

One day, I was browsing the newspaper and I found an interesting advertisement. The International Dating Agency in my hometown of Odessa, Ukraine is offering services for single Ukrainian and Russian ladies. The agency helps women find, communicate with and, if everything goes smoothly, meet and marry the man of their dreams. Men from all over the world have access to an online catalog with pictures and résumés of beautiful international brides. I was simply curious, and submitted all paperwork with attached picture of myself together with my nine and a half year-old daughter. It also required a brief description of what kind of qualities I was looking for in a man. A lot of women posted sexy pictures showing the best parts of their bodies but I wanted to be honest from the very beginning, show that I have serious intentions, a child from my first marriage and that there was nothing to hide from a future prospective mate.

After a short period of time, I started to receive emails addressed directly to the agency whose job was to translate from English to Russian and present the interpretation to me. The fun was almost overwhelming. Raised to be polite, I could not say "no" without at least a couple of exchanges. A ton of email poured in from Sweden, Germany, Spain and America. Almost unbelievable to find out that so many men are desperately searching for beautiful international brides. I was briefly communicating with several men at the same time—back and forth, back and forth, back and forth. Whew!!

Finally, my attention caught an American man who liked my picture because I was in it with my daughter. He told me years later that apparently, it was attractive. The attraction was mutual. I liked what he wrote. His short, informative letter impressed me with very intelligent language, simplicity and transparency. We started communicating with each other through this agency and soon figured out that we don't want anybody to witness our very personal exchanges. I decided to write a letter myself using an English dictionary.

It was not easy. My school program, obviously, was not enough for decent English writing. I've tried very hard. Still, letters sounded somewhat naive and very much like a textbook. But who cares about these details when the most precious thing was the undeniable drive to communicate, to get across my thoughts and emotions. In return, my American friend was doing the same thing using a Russian dictionary and, of course, experienced the same vocabulary shortage. Did not matter a bit to me! So much excitement, and tickles in the stomach! Daydreaming and hoping for magic! We both were on a mission to learn about each other as much as it was possible through the mail.

It was taking two weeks, on average, for letters to arrive from Ukraine to America. We hardly could wait to receive letters from each other. I would check the mailbox every day with anticipation to find the letter with an American stamp. He was doing the same on the other end. Our letters' content was becoming sweeter and sweeter. We exchanged pictures and stories of everyday life events, telling in length about our families, our traditions, and we shared our dreams for the future.

One evening, my neighbor knocked on my door and gave me an envelope saying that the postman needed to deliver in person but I was at work, so he left the envelope with them. When I opened it, there was a letter and a birthday card. Wait a minute, not only that, but in the very corner of the envelope was a fine silver chain with a beautiful vintage locket. He bought it at the Ohio Renaissance Festival. Awwww, how sweet and romantic. Touching. Unforgettable!

How in the world did the Ukrainian post office let it through? This envelope crossed the ocean, was touched by so many hands and still safe. There must be an angel, or spirit guide, or divine presence indeed! My heart was singing, my face was shining, my eyes were sparkling with joy! Not for the piece of jewelry, but because he remembered. He remembered my birthday! Is this happening for real? With me? Or is this just a dream and I am soon to awaken?

Overwhelmed with appreciation, thinking *what to give in return?* I immediately wrote him back, giving my thanks, praises, and I came up with a creative idea. I put lipstick on my lips, firmly kissed a piece of paper, heart-shaped it and signed *From my lips to yours*. Then, on the other side of the letter, I contoured my left hand and signed *Touch my hand*. I stuffed everything in an envelope and mailed it. He was amazed by these innocent expressions of appreciation and wrote back, *I placed your beautiful lips on my mirror to enjoy every morning and evening and often, I put my hand over your hand contour imagining how we touch. Your hand is so small compared to mine. It makes me smile every time. Thank you.*

A year and a half of writing had made both of us known to each other, and had developed a very touching, personal connection. We both kept all those letters. Sometimes, mail delivery was delayed, and I would read old letters to renew the vibrancy of positive emotions—re-read again and again.

And then he called. Unexpectedly! Oh, my God! I can hear his voice, but barely understand anything he is saying. Panicked. What should I do? Just listen? No way! I had to think of something to fix this little awkward situation. Visually scanning around the room, restless, running my hand through my hair, I remembered there was a book with pictures on the shelf. The tour guide for the guests. On the left side was the Russian description, on the right, the English translation. I picked that book. I opened and started to read to him the English side not knowing how else to communicate due to a simple lack of understanding live English language, especially on the phone.

"Do you understand me?" I kept anxiously asking several times.

He was laughing on the other end of the phone receiver. Was it because of my English? Did not seem so. He sounded happy simply from hearing my voice and kept repeating, "Are you going to read the entire guide?" Well, since I did not understand much, I continued until he asked me in broken Russian to please stop. He had to go and promised to call again sometime.

After this phone conversation, it was obvious that it was time for us to meet face-to-face and see how good of a match we are in real life. I invited this man to visit me and my family in Ukraine. We set the approximate time and completed lots of paperwork. I had to get permission from the government office to allow an American friend to visit me. Finally, all preparations are done. He is coming soon. We are all excited and nervous a little. How will things go? Will we actually like each other? Is it going to work? What will happen after this visit?

The time has come. February 14th, Valentine's Day. My mom stayed at home and cooked. It is her proud participation. At the airport, my father, my daughter and I are waiting at the gate. The customs checkpoint keeps all foreign passengers and thoroughly browses through passports and visa documents. Here he is, coming through the door and searching with his eyes. I grab his arm and pull, separating him from a bunch of other people. We all smile, say hello and briefly hug. My father takes his luggage and we follow outside to the taxi that is already waiting for us.

At home, my mom prepares and serves dinner at the table. It was full of all kinds of food and wine. The house smelled like a restaurant and the feast began. It is a tradition to have everything on the table. All you have to do is just keep eating and drinking.

We spent two wonderful weeks together. The connection was instant. We were mutually attracted. I took him to see some great places in Odessa: museums, parks, the Black Sea beach. The weather treated us with warm sunny days, which was very rare for wintertime, especially in February. The temperature at times was reaching the mid-fifties. Unbelievable! Everything seemed played to our favor and we enjoyed this great opportunity to get to know each other better. Lots of pictures were taken to preserve the memory of the greatest times together. He also brought a family album and showed his parents, siblings and their kids. He had two sons from his first marriage, close in age to my daughter. Perfect.

The big dictionary helped us with communication. It became "the love book", its pages so much worn from constant use. We are falling in love. Rapidly. He is everything I have imagined. I am a perfect one for him. We are falling. Definitely. Am I dreaming? No, everything is real. We fell in love.

I have never thought that it would be possible to fall in love again. It happened so naturally. Even my daughter started calling him dad. They liked each other very well. He treated her like his daughter, calling her "little princess." So sweet. So kind. Magic was happening right before our eyes.

He proposed three days before going back to the States. I said "yes." A beautiful engagement ring was sitting on my finger—heart-shaped emerald stone with a little spark of diamond on the side. I guess he thought it through and saw it coming.

We had to fill out immigration documents he brought. Upon his return to the States, these documents will be sent to INS—Immigration and Naturalization Services—in order to start the process of bringing me and my daughter to the United States.

I remember myself as a 5th grade schoolgirl back in Ukraine, when in the hallway, two teachers were speaking English to each other. To my amusement, it sounded so fancy and smart. I was mesmerized just listening to the sound of it. I was thinking to myself, *I wonder if I ever could speak like that?* I wished that I could.

Who knew that years later, life will present a pleasant surprise and I will move to America. I guess it was meant to be, or written in the sky. I never imagined it would happen to me but it did happen.

Arrival.

Have you ever experienced time this way: too many events and changes in a very short period of just one year? It seems at least five years passed by. That was exactly the feeling since my airplane landed on American soil. The land of infinite possibilities and greatest opportunities, opened the door. Everything now was for the first time for me, a huge shift has happened.

My entire world, the way I knew it, has been changed forever. I was born again, now in America. The air was different. I could smell something new, unrecognizable, exciting and anxious at the same time. The vast distances, huge speed and new language, I've never experienced in real life, only in English class at school.

Nobody I really know except for my future husband. Just me and Lena, my 11-year-old daughter.

Our first meeting with future parents-in-law happened on the same day we arrived. They were waiting with anticipation. So did we, my daughter and I. There were lots of hugs, laughs and very funny communicative ups and downs. All we could do at that point was let them talk and show us around. I only kept smiling politely with no clue what they were saying. Nevertheless, the memories are still very warm and cozy.

The first real challenge I had to face is my favorite—the language. At the age of 36, with the Russian vocabulary of an adult person, it was not easy to become basically, a first grader. Emotionally, it was driving me crazy! My ego was pinched. I felt helpless and angry at myself. But my mother-in-law was very kind, loving and patient. No wonder why, she raised four children.

We found very quickly a common ground in the kitchen. She would teach me English by pointing to something and naming it. In turn, I was saying it in Russian so she could learn something from me. In those precious moments of relating and communicating was so much fun, so much emotional understanding and love.

Time goes by. While I was working hard with learning the new language, my daughter Lena went to school, sixth grade, and picked up English in a couple of months. It is very natural for kids. She simply became my competition. Imagine family at dinner table, my husband and daughter are talking about their day at school, at work. But me? What a disaster! Hardly able to follow their lovely conversation. What a shame. Believe it or not, I had tears in my eyes, feeling abandoned and impatient, comparing my daughter's quick success to my slow progress. I know that I am trying so hard, with English language textbooks, dictionary, reading newspapers, watching endlessly Andy Griffith, Ricky Lake and Jerry Springer shows on TV. My husband was not happy about these shows—not Andy Griffith, but Jerry Springer. He told me that I should not watch Jerry Springer, it is not a good example and type of language for me to learn. I, however, was kind of shocked and literally glued to the TV screen in total disbelief of such human behavior. Almost like when you are watching horror movies—not believing your eyes and ears, yet still watching it.

I did not work then. Actually, I did work at home as a housewife—

cleaning, cooking, laundry and TV in-between. One day, when cleaning Lena's room, I found children's library books on her desk. Out of curiosity, I opened one and tried to read, wondering if I could follow the content without looking every two minutes in a dictionary. To my surprise, it was easy and fun. I finished the first book in about an hour. Wow! Eureka! I got it. Somehow, it worked. I simply skipped the words I did not know and continued reading. My mind was automatically filling up the blanks somewhere in the background. It was a progress! My confidence received a good portion of positivity. I felt much, much better.

There was a teacher at Lena's school, Mrs. Carlson. She was helping Lena every day during lunchtime at the school library to catch up with English, so she could be on the same level with other kids in her class. Mrs. Carlson and I met when I was picking up Lena from school. That day, she volunteered to help me with English pronunciation. I began to go to school every day before lunch to spend a learning hour with Mrs. Carlson. Very sweet lady. Her lessons helped me even more and another progress was achieved.

One Sunday, we had a short family trip. My mother-in-law and I were sitting together in the back of the minivan knitting and having a conversation about Lena's success at school. In the middle of it she asked, "Have you noticed?" I had no idea what she was talking about. Then she said that I was speaking English in nice, full sentences without stopping and searching for the words. My eyes filled up with tears, happy tears this time.

This journey began in August of 1998. And today, in 2017, I'm still on this journey, learning, discovering, and continuing to adapt to the American way of life.

Takeaways

1. Whatever happens in our lives has its own reason or purpose.

2. At times, life invites us to write a new chapter.

3. Get on a mission to learn more about the people you care about.

4. Communication takes many forms.

5. Be available to help others meet their goals in life.

11 One Step Closer to Heaven: After Death Communications (ADCs)

Matt Petersman

Are you questioning whether there is life after death? Are you grieving the loss of a loved one? Does someone you love have a terminal condition and you don't know what to say or how to help your dying loved one? Do you want a sign from them after they die? Did you know there is a way to spiritually connect with them? Do you also have a terminal condition called *life*?

My Dad and Father-in-Law

Many years ago my Dad passed away due to congestive heart failure. In our last conversation, it scared me to think I would never be able to communicate with him again. So, I asked him if he would give me a sign after he died—a shooting star, a gleam in my child's eye—anything he could do to let me know he was still watching over me: encouraging me, guiding me, and comforting me in times of need. I was fully expecting a "yes" answer from him. Instead he said, "I don't know if I will be allowed." His answer felt like a punch in the gut. But I felt determined to get affirmation so I told him, "Break the rules if you have to." He said he would. And we said our goodbyes.

I was out of town when he died and I was playing *Chinese solitaire* on the flight home. You know the game, with marbles in every depression except in the center.

After removing about half the marbles, I stopped because my mind was blank—completely worthless. I knew I could not solve the puzzle with my mind in that condition, so I closed my eyes and prayed as hard as I've ever prayed and I asked my dad for his help. As I opened my eyes, I had this feeling that my dad was there with me. I went back to the game and finished it with just one marble, and it was in the center hole!

I've played the game many times but never have I had a perfect game like that. To me, that was evidence enough that my dad's spirit helped me. It was only years later, when my father-in-law was dying, that I realized something more profound—a game of solitaire is a game played by one person, not two. It is not a team game. One could say there is an unwritten rule in any solitaire game to not receive any help. When I told him to break the rules, I thought it was related to some rules angels have in heaven about what they aren't able to do in giving signs to people on earth. Turns out, it was the rules of *solitaire*. My dad helped me and broke the rules, just like he said he would! Even now, I know there was no way I could have solved that puzzle on my own, with my mind in that condition. And that was my sign.

A few years later my father-in-law, Ron, was at the end of his battle with cancer. Our daughter, Maddie, was 20 months at the time and started to put words together. Since Ron, or "Poppy" as she named him, needed to sleep a lot when we visited, Maddie started saying "Poppy sleepy" quite often when she saw him. It was perhaps the two word sentence that she said the most. Knowing the end was near, my wife and I spent a lot of time the last week talking to him about God and heaven. Every day, I would read to him from the book I found shortly after we learned of his cancer, *God, I Want to Ask You: Seven Questions When Facing Death*. I was also reading parts of the *Bible* and *The Purpose Driven Life* to him, and it seemed to comfort him. I know it comforted me, and my wife as well. Just like I did with my father, I asked Ron for a sign after he died to show us that he was still there, looking over us. He said he would.

The morning after he died, Maddie woke up very early (which she never did). We didn't say a word to her, and she crawled into our bed to go back to sleep. My wife and I were staring at her between us and Maddie was staring at the ceiling and out-of-the-blue, she said, "Poppy". She didn't say, "Poppy sleepy", like she usually did. It was apparent to us that she sensed her grandfather's spirit and said his name, letting us know that he is still looking over us. My wife's brother and sisters also received signs from their father and I saw more signs from my dad during the difficult time that followed. I continue to see signs from my dad today.

I was very close to my dad, but I'm even closer to him now than when he was alive. Dying doesn't have to be so sad. For those of you who have lost loved ones, pray and don't stop thinking about them. They are looking after you!

The story of my dad and father-in-law teaches us not to be afraid of asking your dying loved one for a healing sign or message. *Will you give me a sign to let me know you are alright? To let me know you are in heaven? Will you let me know you are always there for me?* Ask whatever questions you feel most comfortable with. Their sign may be something as trivial as rules to a game, or words from your child, but it will be meaningful in a way that ensures you will know it is from them.

Jill and her mom, Judy

Jill is my wife's best friend and hearing that Jill's mom died, was especially hard for me. Jill had known about the magical experiences I had with my dad and father-in-law, the signs they gave me from heaven. While Judy was dying, I had encouraged Jill to ask her mom for a sign from heaven.

After she died, I cried every day for Jill and her family and kept praying that Jill would receive a sign or message from her mom. After a week of praying, as I got in my car, I started crying again and closed my eyes and prayed as hard as one can pray. Before I turned the car on, I asked God to have the song playing on the radio be a song for Jill and her mom. I opened my eyes and turned on the radio. Kari Jobe's, "*I am Not Alone*" was playing, a song I had never heard before on a radio station that I always listened to. The lyrics seemed to fit perfectly as though Jill were singing the song to her mom: *I am not alone. You will go before me. You will never leave me.* I was bawling after the first chorus. For the next couple of weeks, I kept hearing the song on the radio, even when I would only be in my car for five to ten minutes. It seemed every time I got in my car, I heard that song. I finally called Jill and told her the whole story and explained why I felt that this song was for her and her mom. She listened to the song and it made her bawl as well. After some time, I stopped hearing the song on the radio. After a couple of weeks without hearing it, I heard from Jill on Mother's Day. During the church service that morning, her church choir sang "*I am Not Alone*"! Of all the songs that her church choir could have sung that morning, hearing this song—on Mother's Day no less—felt like a clear sign for Jill.

The story of Jill and her mom shows how one can pray for a healing sign or message for a grieving friend, not just for ourselves. Pray for your friends and their departed loved ones. Be open to praying for a sign for them and you too can be a messenger.

Anne and David

I worked with Anne and we became such good friends that one weekend I helped her husband when he was building their house. We went to their wedding and reception in their house and backyard. Sadly, their marriage ended 12 years later due to his alcoholism. Anne and their two daughters had an intervention and told him, "If you want us in your life, you need to get help." David refused, and eventually died from his addiction.

A year after David died, he visited me while I meditated and he wanted me to tell Anne four things:

1. He loves you.
2. He's sorry.
3. He's happy for you (Anne was recently engaged).
4. He wants you to pick the beautiful flowers.

The first three statements were fairly generic, but the fourth was very specific. I called Anne and told her what he wanted me to say, not knowing what the flowers meant. Did he plant flowers for her in their yard and he wanted her to pick them for herself? I asked Anne, "Did he plant flowers for you in your garden and pick them for you every year? Or did he get you flowers every Mother's Day or on your anniversary? Were you supposed to pick flowers and put them on his grave?" I said, "He wants you to pick the beautiful flowers. The feeling of picking the beautiful flowers is very strong. What is it with 'pick the beautiful flowers'?" Anne said, "Oh my gosh Matt, I've been praying for a sign from God on whether I should send David's mom flowers or not. She just had surgery and I was going to send her flowers, but we are not on speaking terms because she blames our intervention for killing David." I said, "Anne, it's not 'pick the beautiful flowers' from the ground, it's 'pick the beautiful flowers' at the store. David wants you to pick the beautiful flowers and send them to his mom!" Anne picked the beautiful flowers she found at the store, along with a loving, handwritten card and sent them to David's mom. She included the story about my dream. Anne and her mother-in-law reconciled and became family again. David wanted his mom and Anne and his daughters to be together. Anne's prayer was answered as well and just happened to be through me. I don't feel particularly gifted as I believe we all have the gift of connecting with our loved ones.

The story of Anne and David shows us that we can be a messenger to others. Many times, these messages come through our dreams or during meditations. If you have a dream about or vision from a friend's loved one, don't be afraid to tell them about it. The dream may not make sense to you, but the message you receive could be tremendously healing for your friend.

Nadine and Derrick

Nadine was a co-worker and I always enjoyed talking to her any chance I had. She had to leave work because her son overdosed on heroin. She sent a letter to her co-workers letting us know about his death. Reading the letter, it seemed clear she was drowning in grief. Later that week, I had a dream about her son Derrick. I had never met Derrick and knew nothing about him. He had four very clear messages for his mom:

1. I'm sorry.
2. I love you.
3. It was an accident.
4. I'm trying to communicate with you but your grief is getting in the way.

I didn't think I would be able to approach Nadine and tell her the four messages from Derrick. How do you approach someone with that kind of information? Well, two days later, Derrick came to me again, this time in a twilight vision. (When I wake up in the mornings, I like to keep my eyes closed and enjoy the twilight phase of consciousness. You are open to so much more because, in that state, and in the dream state, we don't have the rules of space and time. Our dreams can be limitless.) During this second visit with Derrick, he repeated the same four messages and gave me two more pieces of information to verify it was from him. He mentioned a T-Y name to me, like Anthony, Tony, Taylor, etc. and the color, red. I knew the red symbolized blood on someone's hands. I thought maybe this T-Y named guy was Derrick's heroin dealer or someone who tainted his heroin.

I figured Derrick wasn't going to leave me alone, so I reached out to Nadine, gently, about having a dream with her son. She was open to the idea. I told her the four messages (I would bring up the T-Y name later, if appropriate). Nadine asked questions about the spirit world and I gave her advice about having faith, believing, and interpreting symbols. I shared with her the meditation techniques that worked for me. She learned to meditate and pray with God's help and conversed with Derrick many times on her own. She was able to release him. He wasn't able to enjoy the place where he was because of his concern about her grief. Derrick needed to let his mom know that he only left her physically—he is always with her in her heart!

I did eventually mention to Nadine about the T-Y name and the color, red. She reasoned it was Derrick's cellmate in prison, Tony. Tony had initiated Derrick into a gang in prison and made Derrick the "Enforcer". Derrick had blood on his hands.

A year after Derrick's death, Nadine revealed to me that, for the first six months, she was seriously suicidal. I remembered being so hesitant to reach out to Nadine at first and so glad that I did. The story of Nadine and Derrick shows us that anyone can learn to connect with a loved one. Even while drowning in grief, Nadine had an open mind. Learn a meditation technique that works for you to quiet your mind and your sorrow. Ask your loved one questions and listen for the answers. Try not to be grieving too much or you may miss the answers.

Conclusion

So, my wish for you is to reach out to others and share these after death communication stories and your own stories as well. Once you have this unbelievable experience with a loved one, you will want everyone to have that experience, to have a magical relationship with their loved one's spirit. Receiving a sign or message from your departed loved one—to know their essence, their consciousness survived their physical death—can be a tremendously healing part of the grieving process. You can make a difference in someone else's life, so please keep sharing.

Takeaways

1. Through deep meditation and prayer, you can communicate with loved ones who have passed on.

2. An ADC (after death communication) with a loved one can be an important healing step in the grieving process.

3. Learn what to say to a dying loved one. "Will you give me a sign from heaven that you are always with me?"

4. We can be messengers for others. Learn how sharing ADC stories can help others.

12 Living Life with No Barriers: How to Push Yourself Outside of Your Comfort Zone
Matthew Shapiro

The cold Utah air hits my face. My heart is pounding. My palms are sweaty. I look up at the top of the rock wall and wonder how will I get to the top? The rock wall staff helps me get situated in the bucket that will serve as my temporary chair and my harness for this journey. I start fast, pulling up and down on the lever that will help inch me to the top of the wall. I am 20 minutes into this personal challenge. I must be getting close. "Mom, how far up am I?" My Mom replies, "Matthew, you are only a third of the way up." You have got to be kidding me. I keep pushing to get up the wall. I have to get to the top to prove I can conquer this challenge and escape my bubble. I am now 30 minutes in and my arms are burning from all of the pull-ups. I have to take a break. Down below, I hear the crowd starting to give me a countdown from ten to one. I regain the strength in my arms and continue my climb up the wall. I do five more pull-ups. I need another break. The audience countdown from ten to one starts again. More pull-ups. This process continues for a few more rounds. I see that I'm getting closer and closer to the top of the rock wall. I am determined to ring the bell that has tormented me for going on 45 minutes now. I get even closer to the top and I reach for the bell. I almost have it. I do a few more small pull-ups. The chime of the bell rings so loudly that I think all of Utah can hear. I did it. I made it to the top of the rock wall. The feeling of victory rushes through my body. I have shattered my comfort zone.

This story was my experience in 2015 when I attended the No Barriers Summit. This summit challenges individuals with disabilities to push themselves outside their comfort zone and go beyond their limitations. I wanted to attend this event to escape my comfort zone, my wheelchair. I was able to do just that. No Barriers is an experience that changed my mindset both physically and mentally and helped me become the person I am today. The mission of No Barriers is to "Unleash the potential of the human spirit. Through transformative experiences, tools and inspiration, No Barriers helps people embark on a quest to contribute their absolute best to the world".

One of my earliest memories is seeing a picture of me as a baby where my Dad's wedding ring fit on my wrist as if it were a bracelet. I was born 12 weeks premature, weighed 3.1 pounds and I was diagnosed shortly thereafter with Cerebral Palsy (CP) which requires me to use a power wheelchair. For years, that wheelchair became a barrier to me fully experiencing all that life had to offer. The No Barriers situation presented an opportunity to get out of my "bubble" and achieve more out of my life.

My wheelchair was, at one point, my comfort zone and my barrier. I want you to think about your barrier. Are you shy? Are you unwilling to try a new diet that could potentially lead to a healthier life? Are you too nervous to talk to that one person that you have had a crush on as long as you've known them? Whatever your barrier is, I hope that my tips and suggestions will help you shatter your own barriers and attain a new comfort zone so you can experience life-changing situations just like I did. I utilize several strategies to go beyond my comfort zone. I hope these strategies will assist you in your journey to develop a better version of yourself.

A purposeful risk is often worth the reward

Taking any sort of risk can be scary, intimidating, and paralyzing. We don't know what the outcome will be. Will she like me back? Will I end up getting injured or hurt? These are some of the thoughts that run through our heads when we evaluate risk-taking. This hesitation often leads to us missing out on the incredible rewards that come with taking a chance. The argument that I would make is that a purposeful and calculated risk often yields positive rewards. Before I attended No Barriers, I was not really a risk-taker. I stayed in my wheelchair and I was happy. However, through being at the Summit I was shown that if I take careful risks and understand that the purpose behind my risk makes me better, I can then get motivated to achieve my end reward.

Many questions entered my mind when I contemplated taking on the rock wall. Could I make it to the top? Would I be dropped getting into the bucket? Could I get hurt doing this? All of those risks were replaced with feelings of accomplishment, joy, and astonishment when I reached the top. For the rest of that day, I felt like I could accomplish anything and I was on cloud nine. My reward was not only the views at the top of the rock wall, but also the sense of empowerment within myself that I did not let the risk that came with climbing the wall deprive me of those rewards. Don't let the risks outweigh the ultimate rewards you will feel once you achieve a goal. Push past your barriers.

Embrace your discomfort

No one likes being uncomfortable. It is hard tackling a challenge, especially when we have to do it while being unsure or uneasy. However, a strategy I would provide is to embrace your discomfort. Some of the most rewarding experiences in our lives come out of situations where we were not initially comfortable with the scenario. For me, a situation that always elicits discomfort is when I need assistance transferring from one place to another (for example, wheelchair to plane seat). I used to be nervous about these moves for a number of reasons. Because of previous surgeries, I feel sharp pain anytime I am lifted. I was fearful of the possibility of someone dropping me onto the floor. This is not a situation that I care to repeat, after experiencing it several times. Lastly, I was afraid the people who were helping me would be injured. It wasn't until I participated in No Barriers that I began to embrace the discomfort during transfers and trust that the maneuvers would go off without incident. Now, I take a deep breath before a transfer and wait for the quick joyride to end. I learned to embrace my discomfort. As a result, I climb rock walls, scuba dive and fly to all corners of the United States.

What is your discomfort? What situations make you nervous? Yes, I will admit at first it will probably scare you to no end, but imagine if you figure out tactics to embrace that uncomfortable situation. You might find a new passion. There is nothing wrong with a few nerves, just don't let those nerves become so debilitating that you miss out on unique opportunities because you aren't willing to embrace a little bit of discomfort along the way.

Embrace your vulnerability

Going hand in hand with embracing your discomfort is embracing your vulnerability. One of the hardest things to do in life is to completely let your guard down in any situation and allow yourself to be vulnerable. Being vulnerable means giving up control during a time when you don't know how the other party will react or how the situation will unfold.

Showing vulnerability is hard because you are going out on a limb and don't know if someone will be there to catch you. However, if someone is willing to go out on that limb to be completely vulnerable the rewards can be limitless.

As a person with a disability I am often in situations where I am vulnerable. One of the times where I am most vulnerable is when I am doing a solo presentation or show in front of an audience. Despite the fact that this is something that I enjoy, I am still very vulnerable during those programs. Everyone is watching me and the success or failure of my program falls directly on my shoulders. I could let my vulnerability up on stage transform into stage fright or, I could do the opposite, which is what I do in most cases, and embrace that vulnerability and use it as fuel to put on a successful program. Transition your vulnerabilities from being liabilities to become assets, thus allowing any situation to be stronger and more successful.

Optimism trumps negativity

Just like with discomfort and vulnerability, it's all about mind over matter. Our mindset ultimately determines whether we fail or succeed. As you embark on a challenge, no matter how scary it may seem, if you are optimistic and positive that you will succeed, success will more than likely be the outcome. Optimism trumps negativity. I would challenge you to maintain optimism when considering a challenge. If negativity starts to creep in it could become an invisible barrier to achieving your goal.

When I was conquering the rock wall, I remained optimistic that I would reach the top. When the soreness in my body started to occur, I didn't let that prevent me from facing my challenge and reaching the top of the wall. If you ever come across a situation where you find yourself feeling negative, take a deep breath and think about how exhilarating and rewarding it will feel if and when you achieve your mission. Optimism can bring you endless rewards and a feeling of empowerment.

Embracing new possibilities always shines a bright light on any task. Imagine if you started out with the mindset of incorporating all of life's possibilities rather than thinking about what can't be done due to the ambiguous limitations you face. You'd figure out a way to embrace the possibilities of life to ensure that you wouldn't miss out on unique opportunities.

Embrace the possibilities, not the limitations

Take a moment and consider what limitations you set for yourself. Yes, you might have challenges, but are you going to let them define you? I can't walk. I can't do a lot of things without full assistance from someone else. These are my limitations, but I have looked outside of the box and figured out the possibilities that life has to offer in spite of my restrictions. Those possibilities have allowed me to intern in the White House, start my own business, speak in front of many large groups and live a pretty amazing life. I have figured out how to become adaptable so that I can make almost every situation work for me.

To give you an example, I fly a lot. Flying can be a challenge for me because once I am down in my tiny, restrictive seat, I don't move for the duration of the flight and that can be very uncomfortable. To combat this discomfort, I have adapted by traveling with seating pillows to help give me support. I refused to let this discomfort ruin my desire to travel. I challenge you to be creative and come up with solutions so that you can meet your challenges. Look beyond and disregard the limitations that are present in your life.

Focus on your strengths, not your weaknesses

Understanding your strengths and weaknesses is vital for positioning yourself to succeed. Think about yourself. What are your strengths and weaknesses? I would encourage you to put yourself in situations where your strengths outshine your weaknesses. For example, one of my greatest strengths is my ability to talk and communicate, something that can be quite difficult for some people with CP. Knowing this, I have always tried to position myself in scenarios where I can use my voice to do good. That is why I find a great level of joy when I am doing public speaking presentations to large groups.

On the other hand, I know that one of my greatest weaknesses is my ability to deal with numbers. Therefore, I avoid situations where math is required. Through experience, I have found that I do best when using my verbal as opposed to my analytical skills. Figure out what your strengths are and focus on those strengths. This will help you be more at ease in many environments. Do whatever you have to do to play to your personal strengths and to minimize your weaknesses.

Graciously embrace assistance

It is okay to ask for help in life. Everyone needs a hand with something at some point. How you ask for help is important. Some people don't like asking for assistance because they think it makes them look weak. Others assume that it is the responsibility of others to help them overcome bad situations. Neither of these examples is either right or wrong. Asking for help does not show a sign of weakness. In my mind, it shows that you understand that you can't do everything on your own.

What really goes a long way and sets the tone when seeking help is how you approach the topic. Being gracious and polite when asking for help always makes the situation better. As someone who needs help with most tasks throughout the day, I always strive to be polite and respectful to those who offer assistance. I may not always need the offered help, but I act in a courteous manner regardless. The goal is to carry yourself in a manner that makes people feel a sincere sense of genuineness. How we present ourselves often says more than our words and goes a long way toward gaining the respect of others. Remember, it is okay to seek help, but be genuine when reaching out.

Don't let criticism cloud your goals

Criticism is tough for anyone to handle. We all think that our thoughts and goals are the best ideas. The challenge comes when somebody doesn't necessarily see the same vision. They might disagree with your concept.

I have faced criticism many times in my life. I try to respectfully accept the criticism and look for the positives in it. Use criticism as fuel to improve your ideas or yourself. Use criticism as a learning experience. Push yourself to be better. Don't take anything personally. If we allow the criticism to affect our long-term goals, we will be stuck in neutral and never progress forward. Be gracious in receiving criticism and look for ways to improve yourself. How you accept criticism can go a long way towards developing a strong reputation as a team player.

Set incremental and achievable goals

Everyone dreams and imagines achieving their greatest goal. Depending on the individual, this could be something as grand as becoming a professional athlete or something as small as saving money for a big purchase. The biggest challenge to achieving these dreams is figuring out the necessary steps to take in order to attain the desired result. Set incremental and achievable goals and plan your path to get there. When you have a goal in mind, instead of just thinking about the end, sit down and consider developing a plan or a timeline to help you reach that goal. Follow your plan through all of the ups and downs. Revisit your plan periodically.

One of my goals was starting my own business. I had to get organized. I knew I wouldn't immediately go from the idea stage to making lots of money. I planned out the necessary steps I needed to take in order to be successful. This included designing a logo, website, and business plan. Two and a half years later, I am reaping the benefits of a somewhat successful business because I followed a plan and set up incremental steps. Having a plan allowed me to achieve small victories and successes along the way.

Our comfort zones are like warm comfortable beds on a cold winter day. We don't want to go beyond them because we are content in what we know. It is my hope that this chapter has given you some takeaways to contemplate as you encounter difficult situations. I was like you and didn't want to leave the security of my wheelchair. It was what I knew. By using the strategies that I have outlined, I have been able to make a better version of myself. This is what I hope you will do with my words and experiences. Go forward and smash your way out of your comfort zone and see all of the incredible and remarkable opportunities that the world has to offer.

Neale Donald Walsch says, "Life begins at the end of your comfort zone." Explore the world. See what challenges await you. Find your new life at the end of your comfort zone.

Takeaways

1. A purposeful risk is often worth the reward.

2. Some of the most rewarding experiences in our lives come out of situations where we embrace our discomfort and vulnerability.

3. Optimism trumps negativity.

4. Embrace life's possibilities, not its limitations.

5. Focus on your strengths, not your weaknesses.

6. Graciously embrace assistance. Everyone needs a hand sometimes.

13 It Cannot Shatter Hope
Amy Schmitt

Let the morning bring me word of your unfailing love. Psalm 143:8

"My hope is built on nothing less, than Jesus' blood and righteousness…." I remember singing that hymn as a child at the top of my lungs not realizing what it all meant until I became an adult. It isn't until you are facing a tough situation that you begin to realize where your hope comes from. We so often say, "I hope it all works out" or, "I hope they come up with something".

Where are we placing that hope? If we place our hope in people, processes, plans (hmm, the three P's), we are sure to be disappointed. True, we can have all those things in place and hope that it all works out. But aren't some of the best-laid plans…you know the rest. It was quite evident in the Fall of 2014 that my best-laid plans were not meant to be—the hope I had placed in my future was not what He had in mind.

I had always dreamed of owning my own company. I had dabbled in several small ventures, but I felt God leading me to something bigger. An opportunity arose to open a gluten-free bakery in my local area. I was hesitant at first because this meant a large financial investment, a huge time commitment, and an even bigger leap of faith. My husband and I discussed the venture at length. I prayed even more.

We were high atop a mountain in Montana's beautiful Glacier National Park, when it started to come together. There was this sweet young couple on the Red Bus Tour with us that day. The whole while we were traveling Going-to-the-Sun Road, they were dreaming—planning. They were excited. At the top of that mountain, at Logan Pass Visitors Center, I asked them what they were planning. The young man said, "We are opening a restaurant on a boat off the bay in Massachusetts when we get home." I was so happy for them. My husband then said, "Are you going to share what you are considering?" I reluctantly shared my idea for a bakery and the young man said to me, "What are you afraid of?"

October 2014, I jumped in and *Simply*—a gluten-free bakery—was born. It was a whirlwind of activity and excitement. There was a space to prepare—ovens, freezers, mixers, and supplies to buy. It was exhilarating! I was in my element. I was in charge. I had the world at my fingertips. I made inroads with a major regional grocery chain and in no time, I had my products on their shelves. Regular customers showed up from all over, even out of state. There were no other bakeries of my kind in the region. *Simply* had nowhere to go but up.

Then I found a lump. Just six weeks after opening, there was this lump that would not go away. I willed it away. I ignored it away. I begged it to go away. It just would not. After the urging of my oldest daughter, I called my gynecologist. I got an appointment with the Nurse Practitioner—of course, my regular doctor was out. But, once you say, "lump on my breast", the medical community does not hesitate. I had an appointment in only a few days.

Not surprisingly, the doctor ordered a mammogram. I had been going to my regular mammos for years now. When I was in my early thirties, they found a lump. Thankfully, after a biopsy, it turned out to be a hardened milk duct. Nothing to worry about. So, I didn't.

I closed the bakery for a few hours so I could go get my breasts squeezed into a pancake. The technician told me it would probably be a day or so before I heard anything. Back to ignore it away. My mind shifted to everything I had to do at the bakery. This was the day I was to demo my products at the largest grocery store in Lincoln. I had to focus. Then the phone rang. "Hello, may I speak with Amy." And, just like that, I was headed back to the radiology center for a biopsy. That day.

You just have this feeling. It's like this bad feeling that you can't quite figure out, but something just isn't right. I was still trying to ignore it away. Beg it away. Plead with God. But there is just something about the phone ringing after a medical procedure. The phone calls really are the worst.

"Hello Amy, honey. Are you alone?" *Oh, my God. Really? This is how it goes?* "Honey, your biopsy came back positive…." I don't remember anything after that comment, except that I was going to die. In that one moment, my life was changed. I was going to die. "Amy, can you get a hold of your husband? I have made you an appointment with a surgeon this afternoon."

This call came at 8 am. I was standing at my kitchen counter getting ready to go to the shop. I tried to call my husband. No answer. I was shaking like a 7.5 earthquake. I could barely type, but I sent a text message. It went something like this: "I have cancer. Please come home." While I have learned a lot of things through my years of marriage, texting a message like that to your spouse when they are in a meeting, is probably not a good idea. But it got his attention.

Cancer. Whoa. Hold on. That was NOT a part of my business plan. That was not a part of any of my plans. Lord, I just found my calling, right? How could You let this bakery be born and find such early success to only put cancer in my way?

My hope is built on nothing less….

My formal diagnosis came right before Thanksgiving. I had a battery of tests to go through to give my medical team the best information possible. I was scheduled for a lumpectomy in November 2014. I was prepped for surgery and the strangest thing happened. The surgeon took my husband and me to a room, not a surgical room. It was more like a broom closet. He began by saying that I was not going to have surgery that day. The last test had just come in that morning, while I was being prepped, and it showed that I had Triple-Negative Breast Cancer and surgery now was not my best option.

The surgeon had referred me to an oncologist. I saw him the next day. My mind was whirling. Nothing was making sense at all. I still had a company to run. I had a family to care for. What was happening? The oncologist was very direct, yet caring. He was very forthright in my diagnosis. Triple-Negative Breast Cancer presented a whole new set of circumstances and treatment options. In Triple-Negative Breast Cancer (TNBC), the cancer cells do not contain receptors for estrogen, progesterone, or HER2. About 10-20% of all breast cancers are triple-negative. This type of breast cancer is usually invasive and usually begins in the breast ducts. Basically, what this meant was that I was not going to have the general breast cancer fight of lumpectomy, radiation, and Tamoxifen. This was going to be a bit trickier.

I was determined to keep the bakery open. This cancer thing was just a bump in the road. I had faith that I was going to beat it. I began to live in this alternate reality where the cancer wasn't that big of a deal. It was just another thing in my daily schedule. I had to look at it that way. I not only had a family who was depending on me but now I had my customers who looked to me for their gluten-free goodness. Being the people pleaser that I am, I couldn't let ANYONE down. I had to keep going. So, that's what I did.

The bakery flourished. My husband, daughters, sister, and friends helped when needed. On the days I just couldn't make it to the shop, I would leave a note on the door stating, "Closed: Amy Chemo Day." When I returned, I would find notes stuck to the door from my customers. Notes of hope. Notes of encouragement.

I would be remiss if I did not talk about the treatment time, how I felt like crap and hated how I felt. This cancer thing was in my way. I would lie in bed, tossing and turning, just trying to get comfortable. The chemo and meds I had to take wreaked havoc on my sleep. I was never nauseous to the point of constant puking, but I struggled with dehydration and malnutrition. Physically I was shot. Mentally I was exhausted. Emotionally I was spent. This was the fight of my life. The fight FOR my life.

Friends and family were fantastic supporters. They brought meals, sent cards, gave gifts and soft blankets. Most of all, they prayed. I kept everyone updated with Facebook posts. I had people all over the world praying for me. I felt such love. The support gave me courage, strength, and hope.

My hope is built on nothing less….

I just kept going. I mastered my first eight rounds of chemo before having the lumpectomy. Then I endured another eight rounds of chemo and thirty-two radiation treatments. By September 2015, I had completed my bout with breast cancer. It is strange when I think back to that time. I remember feeling relief that I no longer had to go to chemo or radiation. Essentially, I could get my "life" back. But, I don't remember feeling completely well. There wasn't a huge relief for me. Maybe I was just so busy with the bakery that I didn't notice. Maybe the crazy rat race of the appointments, treatments, and medications had become such a norm for me, that when it ended, it was just another thing to cross off my list.

Business was good, but not great. The hit of my not being well was beginning to catch up to us. I did not have the energy during treatment to do all those first year business things you should do to promote and sell. There were ample opportunities, but not the energy or the cash flow to get it done. By November, my husband and I had some tough decisions to make. I was trying to be optimistic about the bakery continuing. My husband was supportive and excited for me. I was declared well! Now was the time to go like gang-busters. I wasn't feeling it.

My hope is built on nothing less….

The bakery had a successful Thanksgiving and Christmas holiday. I was still not feeling it. Something just wasn't right. I thought this was where God wanted me. I thought this was what He directed us to do. I kept praying for direction. On a Saturday in January 2016, I called my husband from the shop. "We are closed. For good." And just like that, what I thought was my dream, ended.

I had my first recall appointment with my oncologist in January. He said everything looked good and that he would see me in four months. I left there feeling optimistic. Then, only one month later, I found a lump— in the same area as my previous lump. Back to the oncologist I go. He assured me it felt like scar tissue and since it was right where a drain exit was from my lumpectomy, there was nothing to worry about. He made an appointment with my surgeon to have this non-cancerous spot removed.

I was standing in that same exact spot and the phone rang. I have since learned to not answer the phone in that area of my house.

Cancer. Again. Yet. Still. Why? In March 2016, I began another chemo regimen with a new plan in place. This time a mastectomy was imminent. I was on my third cocktail (that's chemotherapy lingo). Surely this time it will work. My oncologist was devastated. I think he felt like he had failed me. What he didn't realize is that my hope was not in my treatment, my hope was and still is in the Lord.

What was happening? Everything was a blur. My planner was filled, yet again, with more appointments. Visits to doctors, treatment centers, hospitals—it was all happening again. But the most wonderful part of it all was that I had not lost sight of my hope. Even on those days when I couldn't get out of bed because I was so sick, I would say out loud, "Thank you, Lord." Really? Thank you? How could I say thank you? Wouldn't I be more likely to ask, "Why me? Why again? Why are you making me go through this?"

Instead, the Lord had brought me to this place of serenity. It is hard to explain. It wasn't that I had given up. It wasn't that I was not facing the reality of my situation. I had HOPE inside of me—the hope He had given me. To trust Him, to trust His plan, to believe that He has it all under control.

My left breast was removed on August 1, 2016. Everything happens so fast. Your mind doesn't get time to catch up when you are in treatment. Feeling the need to stay focused on the here and now, I think I forgot to truly think about what losing a breast meant. My recovery was rough, to say the least. I was given one month off. Douglas and I took advantage of this time and made a quick trip to Montana. I needed to get back to my mountain.

My tissues and skin would not heal. About mid-way through radiation, my wound became seriously infected. I had to have yet another surgical procedure and more time to heal. Time was of the essence and I had to finish up radiation or risk having to start all over.

This last round of radiation was the toughest. I was also taking an oral chemotherapy drug while receiving radiation. My body had never felt weaker. I was not only struggling with the treatments, but my mastectomy wound was still not healing. I had this open gash in my left chest. It was ugly. It was painful. I couldn't even look at it.

Fast forward to December 2016. My treatment ended on December 14, 2016. It was a special day. Before my final radiation and chemo treatment, the staff, doctors, and nurses at my Radiation Oncology office all joined with me, my husband, daughter, dad and friends for a time of prayer. Yes, you heard me correctly—my doctors and nurses—prayer. This didn't happen last time.

My hope is built on nothing less....

So, where do I go from here? I have been released again. Almost like a do-over. As I sit here writing this, I have seen both the oncologist and radiation oncologist once since December 2016. Next appointments are not for a few months. This is a true test of my faith. We have collectively decided that I will not do any post-treatment scans. For no other reason than this: my oncologist does not want me to live as a slave to cancer.

He believes that the scans, or the appointments for upcoming scans, do nothing more than cause anxiety. I would worry about the scans for months ahead of time, worry about the result of the scans afterward—it would be a never-ending cycle of anxiety. It took me a while to understand what he was saying, but I believe him now. I will not be a slave to cancer.

I am now to live life, to do all the things I am called to do, to do what makes me happy, to make the most of my life on earth. I am trying to figure out what that really means. Because my hope is truly built on nothing less. I trust that God is in control. He is the master healer. He holds my life, my days, in His hands. I don't need a scan to tell me anything. I have hope in my heart. I have peace in my soul.

Expect to have hope rekindled. Expect your prayers to be answered in wondrous ways. The dry seasons in life do not last. The spring rains will come again. -Sarah Ban Breathnach

Takeaways

1. Understand that healing is a journey.

2. Dig deep and find where your hope is built.

3. Overcome life's biggest challenges with hope.

4. Testing of one's faith is the biggest challenge.

5. Focus, courage and faith combine to produce hope.

6. Life is not necessarily yours to control.

ABOUT THE AUTHORS

DEREK ALAN

We are all on a path to finding or fulfilling our Purpose. Through faith, Derek has discovered his purpose and realized his passion: to serve and add value to others by encouraging them to transform the way they think, act and react with the world around them.

Contact: d.alanceo@gmail.com • www.derekalaninc.com
Twitter: @YourCEO   Instagram: /YourCEO   Facebook: /Derek Alan

DAVID COLEMAN

Known worldwide as The Dating Doctor, David is a highly requested speaker, coach and media personality. He's been honored 14-times as Speaker of the Year and is the only speaker ever named Entertainer of the Year. A versatile talent, David's appearances span genres including colleges, corporations, all branches of our military service and civic organizations nationwide. He is the Co-Founder of the MasterMind Coaching Weekend Series that inspired the creation of this book.

Contact: 513-403-7399 • David@DavidColemanSpeaks.com
www.DatingDoctor.com • www.DavidColemanSpeaks.com

LENNY DAVE

Lenny Dave is a nationally recognized comedy historian who entertains and informs a wide variety of audiences–and he's been doing so for 30 years! In 2014, Lenny was selected as the featured speaker (and the only speaker) to perform in the inaugural season of the Red Skelton Entertainment Series.

Contact: 100yearsofcomedy@gmail.com • www.LennyDave.com

BARRY FIDELMAN

Raised in the environment of the family's *Fidelman's Resort* in South Haven, Michigan, Barry started working there when he was 10 years old. He later served as the company's president and then became a real estate developer. Barry is a perceptive student of human nature. Whether on the golf course or in his community, Barry's advice is on the money.

Contact: Fideland46@yahoo.com

ERIN MCCAMLEY

Erin McCamley is a music director, performer, composer, educator, and activist. She believes strongly in empowering young people through the arts to fight oppression, bigotry, and hate. Erin is a co-writer and performer of *She's Crazy: Mental Health and Other Myths*, which she tours with her mother Sherry and friend Cathy reducing stigma surrounding mental illness. She is also writing a show called *She's Lying*, which raises awareness of sexual violence on college campuses and throughout the world.

Contact: erinmccamley@gmail.com • www.erinmccamley.weebly.com

SHERRY MCCAMLEY

Sherry McCamley is a singer-songwriter-musician-actor-director-teacher. She has directed and performed in dozens of productions coast to coast, including *She's Crazy: Mental Health & Other Myths*, an interactive musical created to increase awareness and reduce stigma surrounding mental illness. She has a CD of original songs called *Changing My Point of View* on iTunes.

Contact: sherrymccamley@gmail.com

MATT PETERSMAN

Since surviving a near death experience in 2006, Matt's spiritual dreams and visions have helped many deal with their own personal grief. His passion for helping others in their spiritual journey lead him to co-found the Cincinnati chapter of IANDS (International Association for Near Death Studies). His spiritual connection is remarkably strong and has led him to create the website, **OneStepCloserToHeaven.com**, to help many handle grief and loss in their life.

Contact: Matt.Petersman@gmail.com • OneStepCloserToHeaven.com

LUDA PIRRMANN

Born and raised in Ukraine, I had no idea that my adjustment to life in America could actually become a chapter of this book. Back in Ukraine, after high school graduation, I worked at a factory and studied at a college in the evenings. I now work in accounting full-time, but my adventurous nature is always in search of something unique. So, I got involved in stand-up comedy. Recently, I started writing and performing for locally hosted open mic shows. My authentic Ukrainian accent makes people laugh.

Contact: zenas273@gmail.com

AMY SCHMITT

Amy Schmitt has overcome adversities which have taught her life-lessons about love, life, faith and trust. Her most recent battle against cancer is challenging her to dream big. Her deep faith is her rock. She is surrounded by her loving family and four loyal dogs.

Contact: amylynne1968@gmail.com

EVE SHAPIRO

Eve Shapiro lives in Virginia. She is the mother of two sons, one who is a young man with cerebral palsy. In her free time, she does freelance work for various entities and helps her son Matthew with his disability consulting company. Her hobbies include reading and enjoying her family.

Contact: shapshap1@aol.com • Facebook: /Eve Staples Shapiro

MATTHEW SHAPIRO

Matthew Shapiro resides in Virginia. He is a Consultant and Public Speaker with 6 Wheels Consulting, LLC. It is 6 Wheels' goal to work with businesses of all types to advance their understanding of disability culture. He enjoys learning about politics, watching sports, and hanging out with his dog, VP.

Contact: (804)-317-0819 • matthew.shapiro@6wheelsconsulting.com
Facebook: /6WheelsConsultingLLC • Twitter: @ 6WConsulting

SHERRY M. WINN

Coach Winn is a motivational speaker, a two-time Olympian, a national championship coach, and an Amazon Best Seller. In 2016, she was recognized as one of the top THREE trainers from the #1 Training Company in the U.S. She has written five books including, *Unleash the Winner within You: A Success Game Plan for Business, Leadership and Life.*

Contact: coachwinn@coachwinnspeaks.com • www.coachwinnspeaks.com
Facebook: /coachwinnspeaks • Twitter: @coachwinnspeaks

DR. FRANK WOOD

Dr. Frank, Founder and CEO of **Thriving with Stress**, holds a PhD in Clinical Psychology and works as a psychologist along with being a coach, friend and kayaker. His innovative, cutting-edge training course is designed to manage and mitigate stress in the workplace, in relationships and in life. His work helps those he trains to communicate with impact, both in speaking and in hearing.

Contact: Drfrank@thrivingwithstress.com

ORDERING INFORMATION

To order discounted bulk quantities of

Please contact David Coleman, David@DavidColemanSpeaks.com
DavidColemanSpeaks.com • 513.403.7399

Consider These Important Uses & Applications:

- ☑ *Counselors & Therapists:* For your clients/patients
- ☑ *Campus Wellness Center:* For your students/patients
- ☑ *Medical Professionals:* For your waiting room tables
- ☑ *Meeting & Event Planners:* For your next conference
- ☑ *Educators (Higher Ed.):* For your class/group reading
- ☑ *Human Resources:* For your company employees
- ☑ *Clergy/Faith:* For your congregation members' needs
- ☑ *Senior Adult Communities:* For your library shelves
- ☑ *Book Club:* For your next, meaningful read